It's another Quality Book from CGP

This book is for anyone doing AQA B GCSE History.

Whatever subject you're doing, it's the same old story — there are lots of facts and you've just got to learn them. GCSE History is no different.

Happily, this CGP book gives you all that important information as clearly and concisely as possible.

There's even a section to help you score full marks for your spelling, punctuation and grammar.

What CGP is all about

Our sole aim here at CGP is to produce the highest quality books — carefully written, immaculately presented, and dangerously close to being funny.

Then we work our socks off to get them out to you — at the cheapest possible prices.

CONTENTS

PART ONE: INTERNATIONAL RELATIONS

We've included the most popular options for AQA B GCSE History — you'll need to check with your teacher which topics you should revise for your exams.

PART TWO: DEPTH STUDIES

Tension Builds — 1900-1914

Europe was drifting towards a <u>major war</u> — and Germany and Britain played a big part.

Germany and Britain began an Arms Race

1) The Kaiser wanted Germany to be a <u>major world power</u>, but he needed a <u>bigger navy</u>. Germany began to follow a policy known as '<u>Weltpolitik</u>' — a more <u>aggressive</u> foreign policy aimed at increasing <u>military strength</u> and expanding <u>Germany's empire</u>.

2) Between 1900 and 1914 Germany attempted to <u>double the size</u> of its <u>navy</u>.

3) Britain had a policy called the <u>Two Power Standard</u> — the Royal Navy always had to be as big as the <u>next two</u> strongest navies in Europe <u>put together</u>. It meant Britain would <u>never</u> be outnumbered at sea.

4) Britain <u>responded</u> to Germany's improvements in 1906 by building the first <u>Dreadnought</u> — a new and superior kind of battleship.

5) Germany built its <u>own version</u> in 1907-8 — but, by 1912, Britain had a new, <u>bigger kind</u>.

6) By 1914 Britain had <u>29</u> Dreadnoughts and Germany had <u>17</u>.

The Major Powers made Plans for War

1) Faced with enemies on both its eastern and western borders, Germany came up with the <u>Schlieffen Plan</u> in 1905. The plan was that in a war, Germany could <u>defeat France</u> before Russia mobilised, and then <u>fight Russia</u> afterwards.

2) France prepared <u>Plan 17</u> to recapture Alsace and Lorraine from Germany.

3) Britain created the <u>British Expeditionary Force</u> (<u>BEF</u>) of 150 000 men, ready to travel immediately to Europe in case of war. The <u>Territorial Army</u> was also set up.

4) Russia started to <u>build up</u> its army in 1909 in case of war.

There were Two Crises over Morocco

The Moroccan Crisis 1905-6

1) Morocco was an <u>uncolonised</u> African country, but France wanted to <u>add</u> it to its empire.

2) Germany <u>objected</u> — and demanded an <u>international conference</u> on Morocco's future.

3) At the <u>Algeciras Conference</u> in 1906, Germany was forced to <u>back down</u> by British, Italian, Russian and Spanish <u>support</u> for France taking control of Morocco's police and banks.

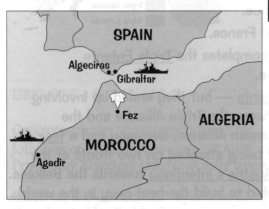

The Agadir Crisis 1911

1) The French <u>sent troops</u> to Fez to fight Moroccan rebels.

2) Germany <u>accused</u> France of trying to take complete control over Morocco.

3) Germany <u>sent a warship</u> called the '<u>Panther</u>' to Agadir, hoping to <u>force France</u> to give them the French Congo.

4) Britain was worried that Germany might build a <u>naval base</u> at Agadir, which would <u>threaten</u> key British sea routes — so Britain <u>also sent</u> warships.

5) Germany <u>backed down</u> and recognised French influence in Morocco. The Germans felt increasingly <u>anti-British</u>.

Countdown to conflict — only a matter of time...

There you go then, three major factors in the start of the First World War. As soon as the <u>arms race</u> began, it was clear a war was possible — Germany was trying to overtake British power.

Trouble in the Balkans

The Balkans were known as 'the powder keg of Europe' — a spark of trouble could mean chaos.

The Balkans were Controlled by the Turkish Empire

1) The Balkans were a very poor area of south-eastern Europe.
2) The Turkish Empire (also known as the Ottoman Empire) was very weak. It suffered from increasing corruption and the rise of nationalism among many of the countries it controlled. People called it 'the Sick Man of Europe'.

The Balkans 1912 (before the First Balkan War)

Other powers wanted Influence

1) GERMANY wanted to build a railway to the East through the Balkans.
2) AUSTRIA-HUNGARY wanted to stop Serbia from stirring up the Slavic people inside its own lands. The Slavs wanted independence and hoped Serbia (a Slavic country) would help them.
3) RUSSIA is also a Slavic country. It wanted sea access from the Black Sea to the Mediterranean, through straits controlled by the Turkish Empire.
4) ITALY wanted to control the other side of the Adriatic Sea.

In 1908 Austria-Hungary annexed Bosnia & Herzegovina

1) Austria-Hungary had been given control of Bosnia by an 1878 treaty. They wanted to make it an official part of their empire. They cut a deal with Russia — who would support this 'annexation' if Austria-Hungary backed Russian hopes of getting access for its warships through the Turkish Straits.
2) Russia didn't get what it wanted, as other powers stood against it — but Austria-Hungary went ahead with the annexation. Russia protested, but Germany, Austria-Hungary's ally, backed them. Russia wasn't strong enough to intervene against them both. This left Russia feeling angry and humiliated.

Two Wars created more tensions

The First Balkan War

Greece, Bulgaria, Serbia and Montenegro formed the Balkan League and attacked the Turkish Empire in 1912. The Turks were beaten easily and were driven out of the Balkan area and forced to give up their lands.

The Balkans after the Second Balkan War (note increased size of Serbia)

The Second Balkan War

In 1913 the Balkan League quarrelled — Bulgaria went to war with Greece and Serbia. Turkey and Romania joined the Greek and Serbian side and Bulgaria was soon defeated — losing land to the four victors.

In both of these wars, the British tried to keep the peace, instead of supporting Russia, who was on Serbia's side. Germany saw this as a sign that the Triple Entente was weak.

There'll be more trouble in the Balkans...

Tension in the Balkans was a main cause of World War One. The Slav question is key here — Serbia wanted to unite the Slavs in the region and was angry about the annexation of Bosnia.

10

Problems with the League of Nations

From the start, the League of Nations had real problems.

The USA Didn't Join the League

Wilson was very ill by this time, and Congress rejected the League.
The USA never became a member. Learn these reasons why:
1) The people of America hadn't liked the Versailles treaty, and refused to accept it. They thought the League of Nations was connected to it.
2) They believed it would be too expensive — many people wanted to stay out of Europe, and wanted only to worry about American affairs. This attitude was called isolationism.
3) Many thought that all people should be free under democracy. They weren't willing to be dragged into wars to help countries like Britain and France keep undemocratic colonies.
4) Wilson's political enemies wanted to make him unpopular, and get rid of him.

The League Wasn't Powerful Enough

1) Britain and France were in charge, but neither country was strong enough after the war to do the job properly.
2) Economic and military sanctions could only work if a powerful nation like the USA was applying them. Most countries were too busy rebuilding to be able to apply them.
3) Germany and communist Russia were not allowed to be members when the League was first formed.
4) The League had no army of its own, and most members didn't want to commit troops to war. Some countries like Italy were quite prepared to ignore the League.
5) The organisation was a disaster — in the Assembly and the Council everyone had to agree before anything could happen. The Court of Justice had no powers to make a country act.

Two Conflicts caused the League Problems in 1923

THE CORFU INCIDENT
1) The Italian leader Mussolini occupied the Greek island of Corfu in 1923 after the murder of an Italian diplomat.
2) Mussolini demanded financial compensation and an apology from Greece.
3) The League demanded that the money should be paid to them, not Italy.
4) But Mussolini got the decision overturned and received the money and the apology he wanted. The League looked weak.

FRENCH OCCUPATION OF THE RUHR
1) Germany failed to keep up with its reparation payments.
2) In retaliation, France invaded and occupied an industrial region of Germany called the Ruhr in 1923.
3) The League of Nations didn't intervene.
4) The United States helped resolve the situation with the Dawes Plan (see p.50).
5) France withdrew from the Ruhr in 1925.

Big problems — hardly the Premier League...

The League was doomed from the start, I'm afraid — but you need to be able to argue for the good and the bad sides of the League. The biggest problem it had was when the USA didn't join — even though the idea had come from the US President in the first place.

The Effects of the Great Depression

1929 saw the beginning of a global economic depression — this made the work of the League of Nations a lot more difficult.

The American Stock Market Crashed in 1929

1) In the 1920s, the USA was the most prosperous country in the world, with high wages and mass production of goods. The 'Booming Twenties' saw billions of dollars loaned by the USA to help European countries recover from the effects of the First World War. American companies were selling lots of goods, so people borrowed money to buy shares in them.

2) But problems started to emerge. Many American producers overproduced — there was too much supply and not enough demand. There was competition from countries like Japan.

3) In 1929, the American stock market crashed — people realised some companies were doing badly and rushed to sell their shares.

4) Wall Street is the USA's financial centre where stocks and shares are traded — by October 1929 the selling was frantic, and prices dropped because people no longer wanted to buy shares at high prices.

5) Businesses collapsed and thousands of people were ruined — by the end of the month they were selling shares for whatever they could get for them. This was the start of the Great Depression — a global economic downturn.

The Depression caused big problems in America

1) In 1929 the USA stopped lending money abroad and called in its loans.
2) By 1930 nearly 2000 banks collapsed as people rushed to withdraw savings.
3) Three years later there were over 12 million people unemployed in the USA.

The Depression Affected other Industrial Countries

1) Most industrial countries were affected — banks failed, industries struggled, and trade ground to a halt. The least affected country was the USSR, which had a communist system.

2) Within three years there were over 2.5 million people unemployed in Britain, and more than 30 million unemployed in the industrial countries of the West.

3) Germany, which had relied on American loans, was particularly badly affected, with banks failing, exports suffering and unemployment rising to over 6 million Germans by 1932.

The Depression made the League's work more Difficult

1) The Depression caused widespread poverty. People were more likely to support extreme right-wing leaders — hoping they'd provide strong government.

2) In 1933, the Nazis, led by Hitler, were elected in Germany. The Nazis wanted to defy the League of Nations by overturning the Treaty of Versailles.

3) The Depression meant that countries like Britain and France were less willing to help the League by getting involved in resolving international conflicts. They wanted to concentrate on dealing with domestic problems like unemployment.

4) The Depression was also a factor in some international conflicts, e.g. the Manchurian Crisis (see p.12).

The Wall Street crash — a depressing subject...

You don't need to know the depression inside-out for this topic — but it's important background as it had such a huge impact. Without it the 1930s and 1940s would have been very different.

The Failure of the League of Nations

It's important to see <u>why</u> the idea of the League of Nations <u>didn't work</u>.

The League Didn't Achieve its original Aims

The League set out to prevent <u>aggression</u>, to encourage <u>cooperation</u>, to work towards <u>disarmament</u> and to prevent a major <u>war</u> breaking out again. In the end, it failed on all these.

The League did have some <u>success</u> in improving the lives of ordinary people around the world — combating slavery and poor working conditions — but this <u>wasn't</u> its main purpose.

There are Arguments in Defence of the League...

It was always going to be tough...
1) Once the USA <u>refused to join</u>, Britain and France had a very difficult task — when they <u>weren't</u> that <u>strong</u> themselves. You can't enforce sanctions if nobody else wants to do it.
2) The global economic <u>depression</u> made the political situation <u>tougher</u> worldwide (see p.11) — it was nobody's fault.
3) <u>No organisation</u> could have <u>stopped</u> leaders like Mussolini or Hitler peacefully. Italy and Germany were members themselves, and could have worked harder for the League instead of against it. The same was true of Japan.
4) The League of Nations had to <u>defend</u> a settlement made after World War I which many of the nations themselves thought was <u>unfair</u>.

...and there are Arguments Against the League

It made some big mistakes...
1) The <u>Manchurian Crisis</u> was the turning point — the League should have <u>resisted</u> Japan.
2) Too many members <u>didn't</u> keep to the <u>rules</u>. When they were attacked for it, they simply <u>left</u> the League, e.g. Germany and Japan in 1933, Italy in 1937.
3) Britain and France <u>didn't lead strongly</u>, and were often very <u>slow</u> to do things.
4) Members of the League who could have <u>opposed</u> aggression <u>didn't</u> want to <u>risk</u> a war.
5) <u>Ambitious</u> members like Hitler and Mussolini <u>weren't dealt with</u> strongly enough.
6) Instead of cooperation, it let the old system of secret <u>alliances</u> creep back.

For

- Early successes in preserving peace between minor powers
- Helped to rebuild Europe and aid refugees of the war
- Improved health and labour conditions around the world
- Kellogg-Briand Pact 1928
- Provided the groundwork for the United Nations

Against

- Rise of dictators
- Manchurian crisis 1931
- Failed to force countries to disarm
- Germany and Japan leave 1933
- Abyssinian crisis 1935
- Rome-Berlin Axis 1936
- German aggression
- Italy leaves 1937
- USSR expelled from League 1939
- Powerless to prevent World War II

For and against — now you be the judge...

Make sure you know the League's <u>original aims</u> and can give your own verdict on whether the League can be <u>blamed</u> for its problems, or if they were <u>unavoidable</u>.

Revision Summary

Time for some magnificent mind-bending questions yet again — just so you know how you're getting on. The important thing is to see what you know and to work out what you don't. Then go back over the section and have another go at these spiffing questions. Keep at it until you can get every single one of them right — I know it sounds much too hard, but you can do it... It's the only way to win yourself top marks when the exams come around.

1)   On what date did the fighting end in the First World War?

2)   Who were the 'big three' who led the talks at Versailles?

3)   Which of the big three wanted Germany punished most?

4)   Who came up with the Fourteen Points?

5)   When was the Treaty of Versailles signed?

6)   Which area of Germany was demilitarised?

7)   What was Article 231 of the Versailles Treaty?

8)   What size armed forces was Germany allowed?

9)   How much was Germany expected to pay in damages? What were the payments called?

10) What were 'mandates'?

11) Give three reasons why the Treaty of Versailles could be seen as fair.

12) Give three reasons why the Treaty of Versailles could be seen as too harsh.

13) Explain why the Germans hated the Treaty of Versailles.

14) List the four main aims of the League of Nations.

15) Which countries were permanent members of the Council?

16) Name three early successes which the League enjoyed.

17) Give four reasons why the USA would not accept membership of the League of Nations.

18) Why did Britain and France find it difficult to lead the League?

19) Which two important nations apart from the USA were not members at the beginning?

20) Write brief notes to show the importance of the Corfu Incident in 1923.

21) Why did the French occupy the Ruhr in 1923?

22) Give three ways in which the Great Depression affected industrial countries other than the USA.

23) Why did the USA see Japan as a threat?

24) Why did Japan invade Manchuria?

25) Why did the Manchurian crisis make the League of Nations look weak?

26) Who was the leader of the Fascist Party in Italy in the 1920s?

27) Give four reasons why Italy invaded Abyssinia in 1935.

28) Why did the Abyssinian crisis make the League of Nations appear weak?

29) Who signed the Pact of Steel?

30) Give four reasons why the work of the League of Nations was difficult.

31) Give four ways in which the League of Nations could be judged a failure.

Hitler's Foreign Policy

Hitler rose to power during a time of depression and international tensions in Europe — and his aggressive foreign policy just made things worse...

The atmosphere in Europe was Tense

1) All the League of Nations' attempts at disarmament had failed.
2) Democracy had collapsed in much of Europe. Several countries were led by aggressive leaders who wanted to take over new territories, and weren't worried about defying the League of Nations.
3) Italy and Japan both invaded other countries' territory (see p.12-13) — and the League of Nations did virtually nothing to stop them.
4) Germany still resented its treatment after the First World War.
5) France had never stopped distrusting Germany.
6) Britain didn't want to get dragged into a war, whatever the reason.

German discontent helped Hitler rise to Power

1) During the Depression, extremist parties flourished. There was widespread poverty and unemployment — people wanted strong leadership.
2) Adolf Hitler, the leader of the Nazi Party, got to power in Germany in 1933.
3) The main aims of Hitler's foreign policy were:

1) He wanted the Versailles Treaty to be overturned. Hitler hated the treaty which he saw as unfairly weakening Germany (see p.8).
2) He wanted rearmament. Germany had been forced to reduce its armed forces under the Versailles Treaty. Hitler wanted Germany to be a strong military power.
3) He wanted all German-speaking peoples to be united in a German Reich (empire). This would mean annexing Austria, and taking territory from Poland and Czechoslovakia which had German minorities. This idea was known as Grossdeutschland — meaning "Great Germany".
4) He wanted to expand Germany's territory by taking land from peoples he saw as inferior, such as the Slavs in the east of Europe. This expansion would provide more Lebensraum (which means "living space") for the German people.

Hitler Prepared for German Expansion

1) In 1933, Hitler withdrew Germany from the League of Nations' Disarmament Conference. He later withdrew Germany from the League of Nations itself.
2) In 1934, Hitler agreed a 10-year friendship pact with Poland — which had the effect of weakening Poland's alliance with France.
3) In March 1935, he brought in military conscription in Germany — breaking the terms of the Versailles Treaty. This was condemned by France, Britain and Italy.
4) In June 1935, Hitler reached a naval agreement with Britain. It allowed Germany to build up to 35% of British naval strength and up to 45% of its submarine strength. This agreement implied that Germany had a right to rearm — breaking the Treaty of Versailles.

Hitler didn't lack ambition...

Hitler was an ambitious and ruthless leader. He wanted to make Germany a strong military power which could dominate Europe — and didn't care if he broke the rules to do it.

The Rhineland & Austria

Hitler's foreign policy became increasingly aggressive...

Hitler's first Territorial Success was in the Saar

1) The Saar was an industrialised region of Germany about 30 miles wide, bordering France.
2) Under the Treaty of Versailles, the Saar was put under the control of the League of Nations for 15 years from 1920. The plan was for the territory's status to be decided by popular vote in 1935.
3) In the January 1935 plebiscite (referendum), 90% of voters chose reunion with Germany — showing Hitler's popularity. The Saar was returned to Germany in March.

In March 1936 Hitler sent Troops into the Rhineland

1) The Rhineland was demilitarised by the Treaty of Versailles. Germany accepted this by signing the Locarno Treaties in 1925, which settled Germany's western borders.
2) But the League of Nations was busy with Italy's invasion of Abyssinia. Hitler saw his chance.
3) Russia and France had recently made a treaty against German attacks. Hitler claimed that this threatened Germany, and that he should be allowed to put troops on Germany's borders.
4) Hitler reckoned Britain wouldn't get involved. But he was unsure how France would react.
5) The German forces had orders to pull out immediately if the French army moved in. But France was in the middle of an election campaign — so no one was willing to start a war with Germany. The League of Nations and Britain were angry but refused to take action.

> Hitler was breaking part of the Treaty of Versailles — and no one tried to stop him.

Hitler then turned his attention to Austria

1) Hitler believed Germany and Austria belonged together. He wanted "Anschluss" (union).
2) In 1934, a Nazi revolt in Austria failed, after Mussolini moved Italian troops to the Austrian border, scaring Hitler off.
3) But by 1936, Hitler and Mussolini had become allies.
4) Hitler encouraged Austrian Nazis to stage demonstrations and protests. In February 1938, he demanded that an Austrian Nazi called Seyss-Inquart be made Minister of the Interior.
5) Instead, the Austrian Chancellor Schuschnigg called a plebiscite on whether Austria should remain independent. But Hitler couldn't be sure he'd get the result he wanted.
6) Hitler threatened to invade if Schuschnigg didn't resign. Schuschnigg couldn't take the risk — he and his cabinet resigned, except for Seyss-Inquart, who invited the German army into Austria to "restore order".

> On 15th March 1938, Hitler entered Vienna to proclaim the Greater German Reich. Austria and Germany were united.

The late 1930s — storm clouds gathering...

Hitler was rapidly gaining power — after the humiliations of Versailles, Germany was on the up. Write a list of the main reasons why Hitler got away with sending troops into the Rhineland.

Czechoslovakia & Munich 1938

Czechoslovakia was afraid that Hitler, after taking over Austria, would try the same thing on them.

Hitler put Pressure on Czechoslovakia in 1938

1) Czechoslovakia's borders had been set at Versailles. The Sudetenland was a part of western Czechoslovakia which had a large population of Germans — about 3 million.
2) Britain, France and the USSR agreed to support the Czechs if Hitler invaded.
3) Hitler promised the British PM, Neville Chamberlain, that he wouldn't invade Czechoslovakia.
4) But soon Hitler claimed that the Czech government was discriminating against the Germans in the Sudetenland. The Nazis organised demonstrations in the Sudetenland demanding that the area should become part of Germany.
5) In May 1938, Hitler threatened to go to war. The Czech leader, Benes, was ready to fight.
6) But Chamberlain and the French PM Daladier then put pressure on the Czechs to give concessions to Hitler to avoid a war.

Chamberlain Negotiated with Hitler

1) In September 1938, Chamberlain flew twice to Germany, where he met Hitler to negotiate.
2) But Hitler changed his demands, and set a date of 1st October to "rescue" the Sudeten Germans. Chamberlain called this unreasonable, and the British Navy was mobilised for war.
3) Then on 29th September, Hitler invited Chamberlain, Daladier and Mussolini to a conference in Munich. Mussolini put forward a plan (really written by the German Foreign Office).
4) After discussions, the four leaders produced the Munich Agreement. This gave the Sudetenland to Germany but guaranteed the rest of Czechoslovakia would stay put. Chamberlain gave in to Hitler's demands because he believed Hitler would honour his promise.

> The Munich Agreement was all about appeasement — giving aggressive countries like Germany and Italy what they wanted in order to avoid a major war.

Not Everyone was Happy with the Munich Agreement

1) It seemed like Chamberlain had prevented war. He claimed the agreement meant "peace for our time", and he flew back to Britain to a hero's welcome.
2) But Czechoslovakia and the USSR weren't invited to the Munich Conference. So the Czechs weren't even consulted on their own future.
3) And the USSR, who had big concerns about Hitler, were horrified at the agreement.

> Appeasement may seem a bad idea now, but at the time, many people supported it.
> 1) No one in Britain wanted a war, and some people felt the Treaty of Versailles was unfair to Germany — so Hitler should be allowed to rebuild its power.
> 2) Many British politicians feared communism and the USSR much more than Hitler — they wanted Germany as a buffer between Britain and the USSR.
> 3) Britain's economy and armed forces were weak. Some historians say Chamberlain gave in to Hitler in order to buy time for rearming.

Appeasement — "Peace for our Time"...

Make sure you know what appeasement was — and scribble a list of the events of the Czech crisis.

Poland & the Outbreak of War

Most people were glad there wouldn't be a war — but in a poll soon after the Munich Agreement, over 90% of British people asked said they didn't trust Hitler.

In March 1939 Hitler took over the Rest of Czechoslovakia

1) After losing the Sudetenland, Czechoslovakia began to descend into anarchy. Slovakia began to demand independence.
2) Hitler persuaded the Czech president to allow German troops in to "restore order".
3) In May 1939, Germany signed the "Pact of Steel" with Italy. They promised to support each other if war was declared.
4) Britain and France did nothing — but it was clear that the appeasement policy had failed. Hitler had broken his promises and taken non-German lands.
5) Once the Nazis had taken the rest of Czechoslovakia, Britain abandoned appeasement and made an agreement with Poland to support it in case it was invaded.

The USSR made a Pact with Hitler

1) The USSR (Soviet Union) joined the League of Nations in 1934, and signed a treaty with France in 1935 against Hitler. The Soviet leader, Stalin, was suspicious of the Nazis.
2) But the USSR never trusted the French, and couldn't understand why nobody stood up to Hitler earlier. After Munich, Stalin decided to negotiate with Germany to protect the USSR.

3) The Nazi-Soviet Pact was signed in August 1939. The USSR and Germany agreed not to attack each other. They also secretly planned to carve up another country — Poland.
4) They agreed that if Germany invaded Poland, the USSR would get Latvia, Estonia, Finland and East Poland — but Hitler never really intended to let them keep those areas.

On 1st September 1939 Hitler invaded Poland. This was too much — Britain and France ordered him to leave. He ignored them and Britain declared war on Germany on 3rd September 1939.

The Road to the Second World War

These are the three key areas you need to cover in your revision of this topic:
1) Make sure you learn the final steps to war between 1936 and 1939 — the sequence of events is very important and you should practise the different names and spellings.
2) Be clear on the reasons why nobody stopped Hitler sooner — e.g. the weakness of the League of Nations, the policy of appeasement and the secret plotting of the USSR etc.
3) Remember the long-term causes of tension during the 1920s and 1930s — think about the problems caused by the Versailles Treaty and the League of Nations.

Twenty years on — Europe was at war again...

This is really important stuff. Remember — there were long-term causes as well as the short-term ones. Scribble a quick summary of the Nazi-Soviet pact. Then test your memory of Hitler's actions in the Rhineland, Austria, Sudetenland, Czechoslovakia and Poland.

Revision Summary

Yes, it's time for some more revision questions — just what you need to test your knowledge of this section. This is a really important section because it sits right in the thick of the action. All the problems after the First World War and then during the Depression suddenly came to a head. The key is to make sure you understand all of the different causes of the Second World War. Don't forget — it wasn't just one thing but a whole combination of long- and short-term causes. So start by working through these questions. Remember — you need to practise them till you know all the answers by heart.

1)   In what year did Hitler get into power in Germany?

2)   Give the main aims of Adolf Hitler's foreign policy in the 1930s.

3)   Why did Hitler hate the Treaty of Versailles?

4)   What did the idea of Grossdeutschland call for?

5)   What conference did Hitler withdraw from in 1933?

6)   Which country did Hitler sign a 10-year friendship pact with in 1934?

7)   When did Hitler bring in military conscription in Germany?

8)   What was the result of the plebiscite (referendum) in the Saar in 1935?

9)   Where did Germany send troops in 1936? Explain why nobody stopped them.

10) What was the name given to the joining of Germany and Austria? How did Hitler achieve it?

11) What was the name of the Austrian Chancellor Hitler threatened with invasion?

12) Name the area of Czechoslovakia that Hitler wanted in 1938.

13) What was agreed in the Munich Agreement in 1938?

14) What was the name of the British Prime Minister who was party to the Munich Agreement?

15) What was appeasement?

16) Give three reasons why appeasement was a popular policy in Britain at the time.

17) What was the Pact of Steel?

18) Why did the Soviet Union make an agreement with Germany in 1939?

19) What happened after Hitler invaded Poland in September 1939?

20) Outline four causes of the Second World War.

The Second World War

The Second World War was the <u>biggest</u>, most <u>destructive</u> war in history. It lasted from 1939-1945.

Warfare Had Moved On Since The First World War

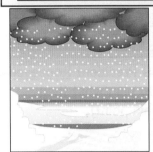

1) This time the fighting really was <u>worldwide</u> — from the desert to the Arctic, from mountains to jungle, on land, sea and in the air. Fighting raged through Europe, Africa, Asia, and the Pacific.

2) <u>Technology</u> had <u>advanced</u> in 20 years — aircraft and tanks had been of limited use in the First World War. This would be a war of <u>rapid movement</u> — without trench war stalemate.

3) <u>Civilian populations</u> were even more <u>affected</u> — by advances in bombing technology, evacuation, occupation, and shortages etc. Many people still remembered the First World War. The <u>economy</u> and <u>society</u> of each country at war were soon geared to helping the <u>war effort</u>.

The Chronology Of The Second World War

| War in Europe | War in N. Africa | War in Asia/Pacific |

Axis victories

1939
September: Germany invades Poland. Britain declares war.

1940
April/May: Germany invades Norway, Holland, and France. Evacuation of British troops (Dunkirk).
June: France defeated. Italy declares war on Britain and France.
August: Battle of Britain. War in the air.

1941
June: Germany attacks USSR (Russia) (Operation Barbarossa).
December: Japanese attack Pearl Harbor. USA declares war. Japan invades SE Asia.

1942
June: Pacific victory for USA at Battle of Midway.
July/October: victory for Allies at El Alamein. North Africa desert war.

Allied victories

1943
February: Russian counter-attack and victory at Stalingrad.
September: Italy surrenders to the Allies.

1944
June: Allies land in Normandy, northern France (D-Day).

1945
February: Allies invade Germany.
May: Germany surrenders to Soviet army.
May: major Allied air attacks begin on Japan.
August: Atomic bombs dropped on Hiroshima and Nagasaki. Japan surrenders.

The Second World War — a war of speed and movement...

You don't need to learn the chronology of the war — but making sure you're familiar with what happened is great background for the rest of this section.

Planning the Post-War Future

The <u>main winners</u> of World War II were Britain, the USSR and the USA. Two important <u>summits</u> were held between the Big Three allies during 1945 to decide on the future of Germany and Eastern Europe. These were the <u>Yalta</u> Conference and the <u>Potsdam</u> Conference.

There were Three Major Decisions at Yalta in 1945

The "big three" allied leaders — British Prime Minister <u>Winston Churchill</u>, US President <u>Roosevelt</u> and USSR leader <u>Stalin</u> met for the <u>Yalta Conference</u> in February 1945 — to plan what they wanted to happen <u>after</u> the war (although the conflict was still ongoing at this point).

1) Germany was to be <u>split</u> into four zones of occupation.
2) <u>Free elections</u> for new governments would be held in countries previously occupied in Eastern Europe.
3) The <u>United Nations</u> would <u>replace</u> the failed League of Nations.

Then the Situation Changed

1) Roosevelt died and was succeeded by <u>Harry Truman</u>, who was <u>suspicious</u> of the USSR.
2) In Britain, the Conservative PM Winston Churchill was replaced by Labour's <u>Clement Attlee</u>.
3) The USSR <u>expanded westwards</u> into the Baltic states and parts of Finland, Czechoslovakia, Poland and Romania.

The allies were now <u>suspicious</u> of each other. Stalin wanted to <u>control Eastern Europe</u> so didn't want elections there — the USA and Britain suspected this. Truman and Attlee were new to their jobs — Stalin thought they'd be <u>weak leaders</u> so he could do <u>whatever he wanted</u>.

Agreements were Made at Potsdam in August 1945

<u>Germany surrendered</u> in <u>May 1945</u>. The allies made more decisions about <u>post-war Europe</u>:
1) The new <u>boundaries</u> of <u>Poland</u> were agreed.
2) The allies decided to <u>divide</u> Germany and Berlin between them.
3) They agreed to legal <u>trials</u> at Nuremberg of Nazi leaders for <u>war crimes</u>.

The USA and USSR had very Different Ideologies

Although the USA and USSR had been <u>allies</u> during the Second World War they had very different beliefs. The USSR was <u>communist</u>. The USA was <u>capitalist</u>. After the end of the Second World War, the two countries became <u>rivals</u>.

1) Economically, communism meant <u>state control</u> of industry and agriculture. The USA, by contrast, valued <u>private enterprise</u> — the 'American Dream' was that anyone could work their way to the top to be <u>wealthy and successful</u>.
2) Politically, communism meant a <u>one-party state</u>. The USA valued <u>political freedom</u>.
3) Communism aimed at world <u>revolution</u>, and so it was seen by Americans as a <u>danger</u> to their <u>democracy</u>. Likewise, the communists feared worldwide <u>American influence</u>.

Yalta learn this page — it's important...

Plenty for you to learn here — things changed fast after the war. Remember two of the Big Three <u>changed leaders</u> — you need to know what <u>difference</u> this made.

Increasing Tensions

After World War Two, the USA and USSR were the major world superpowers. Unfortunately, relations between them went rapidly downhill...

The USA and the USSR began an Arms Race

The USA and USSR became very competitive — each wanting to be the strongest, and feeling threatened by the other. There was an arms race to have the most powerful weapons.

1) Germany surrendered in May 1945, but the war against Japan continued. In August 1945, the USA dropped two atom bombs on Japan — destroying the cities of Hiroshima and Nagasaki. These bombs were incredibly powerful and thousands of civilians were killed. Japan surrendered immediately after this.

2) The USA had kept the atom bomb (A-bomb) secret from the USSR until just before it was used in Japan. For four years, the USA was the world's only nuclear power.

3) But in 1949, the USSR exploded their own A-bomb. The USA developed the even more powerful hydrogen bomb (H-bomb) in 1952. The USSR had followed with their own by 1955.

The USSR became Influential in Eastern Europe

1) At the end of the Second World War, the USSR's Red Army occupied Eastern Europe. Stalin had no intention of keeping the promise he made at Yalta to allow free elections in Poland.

2) Between 1945 and 1948, Stalin installed pro-Soviet "puppet" governments in Poland, Hungary, Romania, Bulgaria and Czechoslovakia. Free speech was suppressed.

3) Non-communist parties were banned, and even communist parties were controlled by the Cominform (Communist Information Bureau) to consist solely of Russian-style communists.

4) Comecon (the Council for Mutual Economic Assistance), set up in 1949, worked to nationalise the states' industries and collectivise agriculture.

5) For a while it seemed that Czechoslovakia might remain democratic. But when the Communist Party seemed likely to lose ground in the next election, it seized power in February 1948.

6) The exception to Soviet domination was Yugoslavia, which had freed itself from the Germans without the Red Army. Yugoslavia was communist but more open to the West. Its leader, Tito, argued with Stalin over political interference. Stalin cut off aid but didn't invade.

There was an 'Iron Curtain' between East and West

- The Iron Curtain

1) Increasing tensions between the USA and the USSR became known as the 'Cold War'.

2) It was called the Cold War because there wasn't any direct fighting — instead both sides tried to gain the upper hand with alliances and plans.

3) Both sides were afraid of another war because of the huge power of atomic weapons.

4) Countries in Western Europe tended to support the USA. Most countries in Eastern Europe were dominated by the USSR.

5) In a famous speech, Winston Churchill warned there was an Iron Curtain dividing Europe.

The Iron Curtain — it just wouldn't wash...

Nuclear weapons were capable of wiping out entire cities in one go — people thought it could be the end of humankind if a proper war broke out, which is why both sides were so cautious.

US Influence and the Berlin Blockade

If there was one thing the USA <u>didn't want</u>, it was for the whole world to go <u>communist</u>.

The USA was Worried about the Spread of Communism

<u>President Truman</u> was worried that other countries might also fall to communism. Truman tried to <u>stop the spread</u> of communism in two main ways:

1) The Marshall Plan

This promised American <u>aid</u> to European countries to help <u>rebuild</u> their <u>economies</u> — West Germany benefited massively. The USA was worried that if Western Europe remained <u>weak</u> it might be vulnerable to <u>communism</u>.

2) The Truman Doctrine

The USA would <u>support</u> any nation threatened by a communist <u>takeover</u>. For example, the USA gave <u>$400 million</u> of aid to <u>Turkey</u> and <u>Greece</u> to try to stop communism spreading. A <u>civil war</u> had started in Greece in 1946 between the <u>pro-Western government</u> and <u>communists</u> — Truman wanted to give the government all the help he could.

In 1948 the USSR and the West Disagreed over Berlin

French Sector

British Sector

USA Sector

BERLIN

Soviet Sector

In East Germany (controlled by USSR)

1) There were <u>four zones</u> of occupied Berlin. The USA and Britain agreed to <u>combine</u> their zones into a zone called <u>Bizonia</u> in 1947.
2) The French agreed to combine their zone with them — the new western zone had a <u>single government</u>, and a <u>new</u> currency to help economic recovery.
3) The Soviet Union <u>opposed</u> these moves. Stalin wanted to keep Germany weak — so he decided to <u>blockade</u> Berlin.
4) Berlin was in Eastern Germany, which was controlled by the USSR — so Stalin ordered that all <u>land communication</u> between West Berlin and the outside world should be <u>cut off</u>.

West Berlin survived because of the <u>Berlin Airlift</u>. Between June 1948 and May 1949, the only way of <u>obtaining supplies</u> from the outside world was <u>by air</u>. By 1949, 8000 tons of supplies were being flown into West Berlin each day.

In 1949 Stalin Ended the Blockade

1) <u>Two new states</u> were formed — West Germany (German Federal Republic) and communist East Germany (German Democratic Republic).
2) In 1949 the Western Powers formed <u>NATO</u> (the North Atlantic Treaty Organisation) against the communist threat. The Eastern Bloc formed the <u>Warsaw Pact</u> in 1955 — a military treaty designed to counter NATO.

Two Germanies — and two German football teams...

Don't forget, the Cold War <u>never</u> led to any real fighting between the USA and USSR. Instead they seemed to be playing a giant game of chess. Make sure you know the <u>two US policies</u> intended to stop Europe turning communist, and the events that led to Germany being split up.

The Korean War

In 1949 the Communist State of China was set up by Mao Tse-tung — this meant that the USA was also worried by the communist threat in Asia.

In 1950 War broke out in Korea

Communist North Korea went to war with South Korea in order to reunite the country — this was seen as a direct challenge from communism to the West. The USA and the Western powers intervened on behalf of the United Nations to stop communism spreading.

The UN Aim was to Resist communist North Korean Aggression

1) The UN ordered an immediate attack against the North Koreans. UN forces landed at Inchon and drove the North Koreans back over the 38th parallel by September 1950.
2) President Truman allowed General MacArthur (UN commander) to invade North Korea — most of the UN forces were Americans.
3) This worried China, who feared a Western invasion.
4) In October 1950, China joined the North Koreans in an attack which drove the UN forces back, and captured Seoul (the capital of South Korea) by January 1951. A UN counteroffensive retook the city, and drove the North Koreans back to near the original border.
5) MacArthur wanted to attack China but Truman disagreed — after arguing with the President, MacArthur was sacked.
6) Truman looked for peace and a ceasefire was agreed in 1953.

Stalin died in 1953

1) Stalin's death was a big turning point. He'd been the USSR's leader since the 1920s.
2) Soviet policy seemed to change under the new leader Khrushchev — he was critical of Stalin.
3) Khrushchev was in favour of peaceful coexistence between capitalist and communist states.
4) He made gestures of friendship to the USA — e.g. he met with US President Eisenhower at the Geneva Summit in 1955, and in 1959 he became the first leader of the USSR to visit the USA. He freed some prisoners and reduced censorship in the USSR.
5) In 1955 the USSR agreed to the Austrian State Treaty, which led to the withdrawal of all French, British, US and Soviet troops from their shares of Allied-occupied Austria. This allowed Austria to become an independent and neutral state (it joined neither NATO nor the Warsaw Pact).
6) This period was called a "thaw" in the Cold War because Khrushchev's policies seemed much less harsh than Stalin's.

The Asian Cold War — pretty hot really...

The Korean War was a dangerous moment that could easily have become a World War — make sure you know the main reasons why the UN invaded and why China fought back.

The Hungarian Rising

After Stalin's death, protests in Hungary led to some softening in Soviet policy. However, the problems were still far from over, and competition with the US continued...

Hungary was treated Differently at first

1) After the Second World War, the USSR helped put Rákosi, a brutal Stalinist, in charge of Hungary. His authoritarian regime became increasingly unpopular.
2) In October 1956, the people of Budapest protested against the government of Rákosi.
3) The secret police, who'd executed or imprisoned thousands of Hungarians, were hunted down.
4) Khrushchev allowed the liberal Nagy to become Hungarian Prime Minister.
5) Austria (which borders Hungary) declared itself a neutral state in 1955. Nagy hoped that Hungary could also be a neutral state.

> In November 1956 Nagy announced that Hungary would withdraw from the Warsaw Pact and hold free elections — ending communism there.

Soviet tanks Invaded Hungary in October 1956

1) Over 20 000 Hungarians were killed.
2) Nagy was arrested and later hanged.
3) The Hungarian government asked the UN for help, but the USSR vetoed the draft resolution calling on them to remove their tanks.
4) Western countries condemned the USSR's actions, but the US couldn't come to Hungary's aid without risking a nuclear war. So they used the invasion as anti-USSR propaganda.
5) Kádár became Prime Minister and ensured loyalty towards the USSR.
6) The incident showed that despite the "thaw" in policy, Khrushchev could still be harsh.

The Arms Race continued through the 50s and 60s

1) In 1957, the Soviets test-fired the first Intercontinental Ballistic Missile (ICBM), and also launched Sputnik 1, the world's first artificial satellite.
2) This new technology frightened the West as it was now clearly possible to launch a nuclear missile attack on the USA from the USSR.
3) But the USA soon made advances. The USA's Atlas ICBM was launched in 1957, and in 1960 the Polaris missile was the first submarine-launched ICBM.
4) The number of American ICBMs increased from 200 in 1961 to 1000 in 1967. Then the USSR began catching up again as American resources were diverted into the Vietnam War. Both sides now had enough bombs to destroy each other many times over.
5) As well as the arms race, there was a space race. The USSR got the first man in space — Yuri Gagarin in 1961. The US launched its Apollo program, and was the first to get men on the Moon in 1969.

For more on the arms race, see p.23.

In Hungary, things got better — then worse again...

Hungary tried to break away from Soviet control but was quickly and brutally brought back into line. This foreshadowed what was later to happen in Czechoslovakia (see p.29).

Revision Summary

Yes, it's time for those awesome revision questions again — I know it's a pain but there's no way round it. It's the best way to test yourself on this stuff. So if you want to get the grades, you've really got to put the work in now. An important thing to remember here is that the USA and USSR were the only countries who were strong enough to be a major influence on world affairs after the Second World War. Make sure you can answer all of these lovely questions — and if you have problems go back over the section until you've got the lot sorted. So get going.

1) When did the Second World War start and finish?
2) Name the two conferences held by the Big Three in 1945.
3) Which two politicians had replaced Roosevelt and Churchill during the period between the two conferences?
4) Was the USSR capitalist or communist?
5) Describe the difference between capitalism and communism.
6) Where and when did the USA use its atomic bombs?
7) When did the USA develop a hydrogen bomb?
8) Explain how the USSR developed a sphere of influence in Eastern Europe.
9) Which Eastern European country was communist but not under the USSR's influence?
10) What phrase did Winston Churchill use to describe the separation of Western Europe from Eastern Europe?
11) What was the Marshall Plan?
12) What was the Truman Doctrine?
13) Why did disagreements occur over the administration of Berlin in 1948?
14) What was the Berlin Blockade, and how did the Western powers deal with it?
15) Give the full official names of the two new states formed in Germany.
16) What does NATO stand for?
17) Who became the leader of China and set it up as a communist state in 1949?
18) Who was the UN commander who was sacked during the Korean War?
19) When did Stalin die?
20) Why was there a "thaw" in the Cold War when Khrushchev first came to power?
21) Who was the communist leader of Hungary in the years after World War Two?
22) In what way did Nagy hope to make Hungary like Austria?
23) Who replaced Nagy as leader of Hungary?
24) What was Sputnik 1?
25) Who got the first man in space — the USA or the USSR? What was his name?

The Cuban Missile Crisis

The USA wanted to keep all countries close to its shores <u>friendly</u>.

Cuba is Only 100 Miles from the USA

Fidel Castro

1) Since 1952, Cuba had been <u>ruled</u> by Batista, a ruthless and corrupt military <u>dictator</u>. Batista allowed American businessmen and the Mafia to make <u>huge profits</u> in a country where <u>most people</u> lived in <u>poverty</u>.
2) In 1953 <u>Fidel Castro</u> attempted to <u>overthrow</u> the government, but he was <u>defeated</u> and <u>imprisoned</u>. After his release in 1955, he fled Cuba.
3) In 1956 Castro returned and began a <u>guerrilla war</u>. By 1959, he had enough support to take Cuba's capital, Havana, and <u>successfully</u> overthrow the government.

Castro wanted to Get Rid of American Influence

1) Castro made a big impact. He <u>shut down</u> the gambling casinos and the brothels. He also <u>nationalised</u> American-owned sugar mills.
2) The USA <u>cut off</u> diplomatic <u>relations</u> with Cuba.
3) Castro began to work with the USSR — he'd always been <u>influenced</u> by <u>communism</u>.
4) The USSR offered to buy Cuba's sugar <u>instead</u> of the USA.

Cuban Rebels in America plotted an Invasion

1) In 1961, President Kennedy authorised a CIA-trained <u>invasion</u> of Cuba by rebels.
2) In April 1961, the rebels landed in the <u>Bay of Pigs</u>, but the USA <u>didn't give</u> them air <u>support</u> as they had promised. The rebels were easily <u>defeated</u> — it was a bit of a fiasco.
3) This invasion meant Castro decided that Cuba needed <u>Soviet military assistance</u>.

Soviet Nuclear Missiles were shipped to Cuba

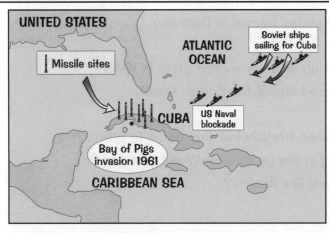

1) In 1962, the USA's U-2 spy planes (see p.29) <u>detected</u> Soviet missiles in Cuba. From Cuba these missiles could be used to <u>attack</u> US cities with very little warning.
2) President Kennedy ordered a <u>naval blockade</u> of Cuba. All Soviet ships were to be <u>stopped</u> and <u>searched</u> to prevent further missiles being transported to Cuba.
3) Kennedy <u>demanded</u> that Khrushchev <u>withdraw</u> his missiles and <u>prepared to invade</u> Cuba. The Soviet ships steamed on to Cuba.
4) The world was on the brink of <u>nuclear war</u>...

In the end, Khrushchev made a deal to <u>remove</u> the missiles from Cuba and ordered his <u>ships</u> to <u>turn around</u>. In exchange the US <u>lifted</u> the <u>blockade</u>, promised to <u>not invade</u> Cuba — and <u>secretly</u> agreed to <u>remove</u> their <u>missiles</u> from <u>Turkey</u>, which borders the USSR.

U-2 were spy planes — I always thought they were a rock band...

The <u>13 days</u> of the Cuban missile crisis were the closest the world's been to nuclear war. There was a <u>stalemate</u> with nuclear weapons because if one side fired, so would the other and <u>everyone</u> would be destroyed. It was a <u>no-win situation</u>.

The Berlin Wall and Czechoslovakia

Yep — even more <u>bits and bobs</u> about the Cold War that you need know...

U-2 was an American Spy Plane

1) The U-2 spy plane was designed to fly so <u>high</u> it would usually be <u>undetected</u>.
2) It meant the USA could secretly get <u>information</u> about the USSR's weapons. It reassured President Eisenhower that the USSR didn't have as many missiles as they claimed.
3) The USSR <u>shot down</u> a U-2 in <u>1960</u>. Eisenhower <u>lied</u>, denying it was a spy plane. But the USSR then produced the <u>pilot</u> (alive) and the plane wreckage as evidence.
4) The USA and USSR were supposed to be attending <u>talks</u> together in <u>Paris</u> a few days later. This summit <u>fell apart</u> because of the U-2 crisis. Khrushchev demanded an <u>apology</u> from the USA, but Eisenhower <u>refused</u> — so Khrushchev <u>went home</u>.

The Berlin Wall was built in 1961

1) Between 1949 and 1961, more than 2½ million people <u>left East Germany</u> for the West through East Berlin. The communist government of East Germany was <u>worried</u> by this trend.
2) So, on 13 August 1961, a 30-mile <u>barrier</u> was built across the city of Berlin overnight. The Berlin Wall was fortified with <u>barbed wire</u> and <u>machine gun</u> posts, and separated East Berlin from West Berlin.
3) Anyone who tried to <u>escape</u> East Berlin was <u>shot</u>. West Berliners were suddenly <u>separated</u> from relatives in the East — for the next 30 years.

> In a famous speech in West Berlin on 26 June 1963, US President Kennedy declared his commitment to <u>protect</u> West Berlin, and his <u>solidarity</u> with its people. Kennedy said, "<u>Ich bin ein Berliner</u>" (I am a Berliner).

Czechoslovakia Rebelled against communism in 1968

1) Alexander <u>Dubcek</u> became Czechoslovakian leader in 1968 and made <u>changes</u> to the country:
   - Workers were given a <u>greater say</u> in the running of their factories.
   - <u>Travel</u> to the West was made available for all.
   - Living standards were to be <u>raised</u>.
   - <u>Free elections</u> were to be held.
   - <u>Opposition</u> parties would be permitted.
   This was called the '<u>Prague Spring</u>'.
2) Dubcek was still a <u>communist</u>. He was careful to reassure the USSR that Czechoslovakia <u>wouldn't</u> leave the <u>Warsaw Pact</u> — unlike Hungary in 1956.
3) But the USSR was worried — it didn't want the <u>Eastern Bloc</u> to be <u>weakened</u>.

4) On 21st August 1968, 500 000 Soviet troops <u>invaded</u> Czechoslovakia and Dubcek was <u>removed</u> from office. Soviet control was restored. Many countries <u>criticised</u> the Soviets, but no action was taken. A UN draft resolution condemning the invasion was <u>vetoed</u> by the USSR.
5) Soviet leader <u>Leonid Brezhnev</u> (who had replaced Khrushchev in 1964) announced that in future the USSR would <u>intervene</u> in any country where <u>socialism</u> was under <u>threat</u>. This became known as the <u>Brezhnev Doctrine</u>.

Communism — the Bloc Party...

The USSR was determined to <u>keep control</u> of Eastern Europe, even if they had to use <u>force</u>.

Détente and the Afghanistan War

After the Cuban Missile Crisis (see p.28), the USA and USSR made an effort to get on...

The USA and USSR wanted to Avoid a Crisis

The Cuban Missile Crisis of 1962 brought the world to the brink of nuclear war.
Future misunderstandings between the Soviet Union and the USA had to be avoided.

1) A telephone hotline was set up between the Kremlin and the White House.
2) The Soviet Union and the USA signed a test ban treaty in 1963 to stop further nuclear weapons testing.
3) Relations between the superpowers still weren't that friendly though. In 1963 the American president John F Kennedy gave a speech in West Berlin criticising communism.

Détente — a period of increasing US–Soviet Cooperation

1) The USSR couldn't afford to continue building up its nuclear arsenal.
2) The USA was trying to end the Vietnam War (see p.97) — an expensive and unpopular war against communists. The US hoped that improving relations with the USSR and China would isolate North Vietnam and force it to agree to a peace settlement.
3) From 1972, US President Nixon and the leader of the USSR, Brezhnev, began a series of talks aimed at improving relations. These were known as the Brezhnev-Nixon summits.
4) In 1972 the two superpowers agreed to limit their nuclear weapons when they signed the Strategic Arms Limitation Talks Agreement (SALT 1).
5) In 1975 the US, the USSR and other powers signed the Helsinki Agreement. This agreement officially recognised the European borders fixed at the end of the Second World War, including the division of Germany.
6) The Helsinki Agreement also included a commitment to human rights — for example, freedom of speech and travel. But since there was no enforcement procedure, these promises were not always kept by the communist countries.
7) China also wanted détente. Its relationship with the USSR had deteriorated, so China needed to gain the US as a powerful ally. It also feared a war like the one in Vietnam with the US.
8) In West Germany, the Chancellor, Willy Brandt, wanted better relations with the Eastern Bloc to improve trade and reduce military tensions.

Talks continued throughout the 1970s with a view to further limitations. President Carter signed a SALT 2 agreement in June 1979 at a US-USSR summit in Vienna — but the Senate had not yet ratified the treaty when the Soviet invasion of Afghanistan altered the political climate.

The USSR got bogged down in a war in Afghanistan

1) To prop up a pro-Soviet government besieged by rebels, the USSR invaded Afghanistan in December 1979. This decision turned out to be a disaster. The USSR got stuck with a seemingly unwinnable conflict in difficult mountainous terrain.
2) American distrust of the USSR increased. It worried the USSR had its sights on the oil-rich Persian Gulf (fairly close to Afghanistan). President Carter warned that the US would use force to prevent outside powers gaining control of the Gulf region.
3) The SALT 2 agreement was being debated by the Senate. Carter withdrew it from consideration, and called for an increase in the defence budget.
4) During the 1980s the USA aided the Afghan resistance with military equipment.
5) Disagreement over Afghanistan led to a US boycott of the Moscow Olympics in 1980 — and in 1984 the Soviet team boycotted the LA Games.
6) The USSR finally gave up and began withdrawing their forces from Afghanistan in 1988.

Revision Summary

Not such a long section this one — but it is jam-packed with huge events in world history.
Make sure you get a grip of the broad outline of what happened, and then fill the gaps with all
the key details. These handy revision questions should help...

1) Name the military dictator who was overthrown in Cuba in 1959.
2) How did Castro set about reducing American influence in Cuba?
3) Where did the 1961 CIA-backed invasion of Cuba land?
4) Why was the US so worried about there being missiles in Cuba?
5) Describe the events of the thirteen days of the Cuban Missile Crisis.
6) What is a U-2?
7) Why did the U-2 crisis cause embarrassment for President Eisenhower?
8) When was the Berlin Wall built?
9) How many people left for the west from East Germany through Berlin before the wall went up?
10) What famous phrase did Kennedy use to express his support for the people of Berlin?
11) What was the 'Prague Spring'?
12) Who was the leader of Czechoslovakia during the Prague Spring?
13) When was the Soviet invasion of Czechoslovakia?
14) What happened to the UN draft resolution criticising the invasion of Czechoslovakia?
15) What was the Brezhnev Doctrine?
16) What does 'détente' mean?
17) What did the US and USSR agree to in 1963 to try and reduce fears about nuclear weapons?
18) What does 'SALT' stand for?
19) Why didn't the USA go through with the SALT 2 agreement?
20) Why did the USSR invade Afghanistan in 1979?
21) Which country gave military equipment to the Afghans fighting the USSR?

The New Cold War

The Cold War had its last gasp in the 1980s...

In 1980 the New Cold War began

The war in Afghanistan and the election of Ronald Reagan as US president in 1980 ended détente.

1) Ronald Reagan was a hardline anti-communist.
   He called the Soviet Union an "evil empire".
2) Reagan was keen to show off American technology and power through
   the development of new weapons — the start of another arms race.
3) The US developed and deployed medium-range Cruise and Pershing
   nuclear missiles which could be launched from almost anywhere.
4) The US also started to develop the Strategic Defense Initiative (SDI or Star
   Wars) for using laser weapons to shoot down Soviet missiles from space.

Ronald Reagan

Poland's People Rebelled in 1980

Solidarność
Solidarność

1) In the early 1970s Poland, under its communist leader,
   had achieved some rise in living standards. But in the
   late 1970s the economy suffered from foreign debt and
   shortages. In response the government raised prices.
2) In 1980 Lech Walesa led shipyard workers in the port of
   Gdansk in protest against the increase in food prices —
   with some success.
3) They set up their own independent trade union called
   'Solidarity' and demanded the right to strike and to be
   consulted on all major decisions affecting their living and
   working conditions. Lech Walesa became the leader.

4) Solidarity became a broad-based anti-communist social movement which by the end of 1981
   had 9 million members. Nothing like it had been seen before in the communist world. The
   movement was especially strong because of the support of the Catholic Church.
5) The Polish communist government was in a fix. It was scared to ban Solidarity — but
   neither could it meet demands for political reform, for fear of Soviet intervention.

The Military seized Control

In 1981 the Polish army leader General Jaruzelski, with Soviet support,
seized control of the country and declared martial law. As a result:

1) Solidarity was completely banned.
2) Lech Walesa was arrested and imprisoned.
3) The price of basic foodstuffs was increased by 40%.

Solidarity lived on as an underground organisation. Lech Walesa became
a symbol of resistance to Soviet oppression — he was awarded the Nobel
Peace Prize in 1983. In 1988 further nationwide strikes again forced the
government to negotiate with the union.

Lech Walesa

Solidarity — rebels with a cause...

There's plenty to learn here. The events in Poland are evidence of popular resistance to
communism in Eastern Europe — which would eventually lead to the fall of the USSR.

The Soviet Withdrawal

Mikhail <u>Gorbachev</u> came to power in the USSR — and radically changed Soviet policies...

The <u>Cold War</u> created a <u>Crisis</u> in the USSR

1) The <u>arms race</u> with the USA was so <u>expensive</u> that Soviet living standards became <u>worse</u> as more money was spent on weapons.
2) Soviet <u>farming</u> was <u>inefficient</u> — there <u>wasn't enough food</u> and millions of tonnes of grain had to be <u>imported</u> from the USA.
3) The communist government was becoming more <u>corrupt</u> and was unable to give the Soviet people the same high living standards as people had in the West.
4) The war in Afghanistan was a <u>disaster</u> — it cost billions of dollars and 15 000 Soviet troops were killed.

Gorbachev introduced Reforms

In <u>1985</u> Mikhail <u>Gorbachev</u> became General Secretary of the Communist Party. He was more open to the West than previous leaders. He introduced two major <u>new policies</u> — <u>Glasnost</u> and <u>Perestroika</u>.

<u>Glasnost</u> meant New Freedom and Openness

The Soviet people won <u>new rights</u>:
1) Thousands of <u>political prisoners</u> were <u>released</u>, including the leading dissident, Andrei Sakharov.
2) People were told about the atrocities committed by <u>Stalin's government</u>.
3) <u>Free speech</u> was allowed.
4) Military <u>conscription</u> was soon to be <u>abolished</u>.

<u>Perestroika</u> meant Economic Restructuring

1) Gorbachev wanted to make the Soviet system of <u>central planning</u> of production more <u>efficient</u>.
2) However <u>corruption</u> in the Soviet economy was too great and he was unable to see through his plans.

Gorbachev changed Foreign Policy

1) In 1987, a <u>disarmament treaty</u> was signed called the <u>INF</u> (Intermediate-Range Nuclear Forces Treaty). The USA and the USSR agreed to <u>remove</u> medium-range nuclear <u>missiles</u> from Europe within three years.
2) In 1988, Gorbachev <u>announced</u> the immediate <u>reduction</u> of the weapons stockpile and the number of troops in the Soviet armed forces.
3) Gorbachev tried to <u>improve relations</u> with the <u>West</u>. He met with the US President Reagan several times, for example at the <u>Geneva Summit</u> in 1985.
4) Gorbachev announced the complete <u>withdrawal</u> of Soviet troops from <u>Afghanistan</u> in 1988.

Gorbachev

> In 1988, Gorbachev decided to <u>abandon</u> the <u>Brezhnev Doctrine</u> (see p.29). He told the United Nations that the countries of Eastern Europe now had a <u>choice</u> — the USSR <u>wasn't</u> going to <u>control</u> them any more.

It's feeling a bit less chilly in here...

By the late 1980s, the end of the Cold War was in sight. Don't forget — the attitude and leadership of <u>Mikhail Gorbachev</u> are the key to understanding why the <u>situation changed</u>.

The End of the Soviet Union

Communism toppled — and the Cold War was finally over...

Communism Fell all over Eastern Europe in 1989

1) Hungary opened its frontier with Austria in May.
2) Free elections were held in Poland in June. Solidarity won and a new non-communist government came to power.
3) Many East Germans crossed into Hungary, through Austria and into West Germany.
4) The Berlin Wall was torn down in November.
5) Anti-communist demonstrations took place in Czechoslovakia and the communist government collapsed in December.
6) In December a revolution began in Romania against the cruel and corrupt regime of the dictator Nicolae Ceausescu. He was executed on Christmas Day.
7) The Warsaw Pact ended officially in 1991.

In 1990 Germany was reunified. Communist East Germany and democratic West Germany were one country again after 45 years. For many people this was a powerful symbol that the communist experiment was over.

Communism was Rejected in the USSR

The main nationalities within the Soviet Union demanded independence, especially the Baltic republics — Latvia, Lithuania, and Estonia. Gorbachev tried to prevent the rise of nationalism in the Baltic republics with military force, but gradually started to lose control.

An Anti-Communist Russian President was Elected in 1991

1) The newly elected President of Russia, Boris Yeltsin, was an opponent of Gorbachev, and became popular and powerful.
2) He demanded the end of communist domination and the break-up of the USSR. This led to a crisis in 1991.

The Attempted Coup of 1991 Failed

1) The old communist leaders feared the reforms, so they decided to get rid of Gorbachev.
2) A military group tried to seize power by capturing Gorbachev, but Yeltsin rallied the Russian people to resist and the army supported him, and the coup failed.
3) Soon the individual Soviet republics became independent — the USSR didn't exist any more.
4) Now Gorbachev had no power and had to resign. Communism in Russia was dead.

The end of communism — when the reds got the blues...

Phew, there's even more stuff to learn here — but you've got to do it. Scribble a paragraph on why communism fell in Russia, and why 1991 was so important.

The USA after the Cold War

After the Cold War ended, the USA had to find a new focus for its <u>foreign policy</u>.

The <u>USA</u> was now the <u>Sole Superpower</u>

1) After the fall of the USSR, the <u>USA</u> was the only country with a military and economy <u>strong</u> enough to be able to take action <u>across the globe</u> — making it the <u>world's only superpower</u>.
2) The USA had the <u>most powerful military in the world</u>, even with post Cold War cuts in spending. Through the 1990s, the US's military expenditure made up <u>more than a third</u> of the <u>world's military spending</u>. No other country came close to spending as much as the US did.
3) The USA's <u>economy</u> was <u>strong</u> throughout most of the 1990s, remaining the biggest in the world while Russia struggled after the collapse of the USSR.
4) This gave the USA a lot of <u>power</u> to get involved in <u>disputes</u> around the world.

The USA saw itself as a <u>Champion</u> of <u>Democracy</u>

In the 1990s, the US tried to be a force for <u>freedom</u> and <u>democracy</u> in the world:

1) <u>1990-1991</u> — The USA supported UN demands for <u>Iraq</u> to withdraw from its <u>invasion</u> of <u>Kuwait</u> and led the UN coalition which successfully drove out Iraqi forces (see p.36).
2) <u>1992-4</u> — The USA led a UN force trying to bring <u>peace</u> and <u>stability</u> to <u>Somalia</u>, which was suffering from a <u>chaotic civil war</u>. But following the <u>death</u> of a number of <u>US troops</u>, President Bill Clinton pulled the US out.
3) <u>1994</u> — In <u>Operation Uphold Democracy</u> the US <u>successfully intervened</u> to <u>restore</u> the democratically elected president of <u>Haiti</u> after a coup.
4) <u>1994-1995</u> — After the break up of Yugoslavia, there was a violent civil war and <u>genocide</u> in <u>Bosnia</u>. The US led a NATO bombing campaign which lifted the Bosnian Serbs' siege of <u>Sarajevo</u> and helped to <u>end</u> the conflict.
5) <u>1999</u> — The USA led the NATO bombing of Serbia, in an attempt to end the conflict in <u>Kosovo</u> (see p.36). While this was a <u>successful campaign</u> — Serbia agreed to remove their troops from Kosovo — <u>civilian casualties</u>, including the deaths of three Chinese citizens, made the US <u>intervention controversial</u>.

Bill Clinton

Clinton also used <u>diplomacy</u> and US influence to try to secure <u>peace</u> between the <u>Israelis</u> and <u>Palestinians</u>, and he played an important part in the <u>Northern Ireland</u> peace process.

The USA still wanted <u>Friends</u> in <u>Europe</u>

1) After the Cold War, Western Europe no longer needed <u>protection</u> from the USSR, so the USA <u>reduced</u> its military presence. US missiles were <u>withdrawn</u> from the UK in 1991.
2) The <u>UK</u> continued to be one of the USA's <u>closest allies</u>, supplying much of the support for the US-led interventions in Kuwait (see next page), Bosnia and Kosovo.
3) Other European countries, such as France, the Netherlands, Czechoslovakia, Hungary and Poland, all contributed to the <u>US-led UN coalition</u> in the Gulf War (see next page).
4) The US was also willing to work more closely with <u>former allies</u> of the <u>USSR</u>. In 1999, three <u>former Warsaw Pact members</u> — the Czech Republic (which used to be part of Czechoslovakia), Poland and Hungary — joined <u>NATO</u>.
5) US <u>involvement</u> in Bosnia, Kosovo and Northern Ireland showed a US <u>commitment</u> to Europe.

There's no one left but US...

Somalia was a big <u>turning point</u> for the US in the 1990s — after the deaths of US troops in Somalia, Clinton avoided using American ground troops in overseas conflicts.

The UN

Even after the Cold War, the UN still had its hands full trying to resolve global conflicts...

The UN tried to get Iraqi Forces to leave Kuwait

George Bush

1) Saddam Hussein came to power in Iraq in 1979. He was a ruthless and brutal dictator, who had used chemical weapons against Iraq's Kurdish minority.
2) In 1990, Iraq invaded Kuwait, its southern neighbour. The UN demanded that Iraq withdraw, and introduced sanctions (a ban on people trading with Iraq).
3) When Iraq refused, the UN authorised the use of force to remove the Iraqi army from Kuwait.
4) In the Gulf War (1991), US President Bush (George W. Bush's father) was in charge of creating the coalition of international forces which drove Saddam Hussein's army out of Kuwait.

The UN used Tough Sanctions against Iraq

1) The UN kept its strict sanctions against Iraq after the Gulf War. They hoped the sanctions would force Iraq to give up its weapons of mass destruction (nuclear, biological and chemical weapons) and stop it from trying to get hold of or make more.
2) While these sanctions helped to cut the amount Iraq could spend on weapons, they hurt ordinary Iraqi people — shortages of food and medicine led to a big rise in the death rates of Iraqi children.
3) The UN tried to help the Iraqi people with the Oil-for-Food Programme — Iraq would be allowed to trade oil for food and medicines. This trade would be carefully monitored to make sure that oil exports weren't being used to buy weapons.
4) While it did help many Iraqis, the programme did face some accusations of corruption — it's believed that some profit was unlawfully made by UN and Iraqi officials.

The crisis in Kosovo was a Big Test for the UN

1) In the late 1980s, the government of Serbia took away much of the independence that Kosovo, a mainly ethnic-Albanian area of Serbia, had previously had.
2) The ethnic Albanians formed a group called the Kosovo Liberation Army (KLA) to fight for independence. The Serbians fought back fiercely, killing hundreds.
3) To stop the violence, NATO began a bombing campaign against Serbia in 1999. After two months, Serbia agreed to remove its troops from Kosovo and allowed KFOR, a NATO-led multinational force, to take control of the region.
4) A UN task force called UNMIK was sent to help get Kosovo back on its feet, helping with policing and reconstruction. But the process was very slow, and ethnic tensions remained, sometimes turning into violence. Local Serbs felt that they were being forced into leaving.
5) There were also reports that KFOR and UNMIK personnel, who were immune from local prosecution, got involved in crime and violence in Kosovo.

A mixed record on fixing the world, UN-surprisingly...

The UN was set up to promote peace and protect human rights. Although, it has helped many people, it isn't perfect. Make sure you learn the UN's failures as well as its successes.

Revision Summary

There's just time for the best bit — some mega-magnificent revision questions for you.
You've really got to test yourself here, because there were loads of facts in this section.
See how many you can answer first go, then look back over the areas you weren't so sure
about. Just keep coming back to those questions — by the time you sit the exam you
should know them backwards... Well, forwards will do. So get busy and get this lot sorted.

1) What was US President Ronald Reagan's attitude towards the USSR?

2) What was the Strategic Defense Initiative?

3) Who was the leader of the Solidarity movement in Poland?

4) Give the name of the Polish army leader who came to power in 1981.

5) When was Mikhail Gorbachev appointed General Secretary of the Soviet Union's Communist Party?

6) Explain what is meant by the terms Glasnost and Perestroika.

7) Why was Perestroika unsuccessful?

8) What was agreed in the INF treaty?

9) What doctrine did Gorbachev abandon in 1988?

10) What year was the Berlin Wall torn down?

11) What year was Germany reunified?

12) What happened to Romanian dictator Nicolae Ceausescu in 1989?

13) What was the name of the President of Russia elected in 1991?

14) Briefly describe the events of the attempted coup against Gorbachev in 1991.

15) What was Operation Uphold Democracy?

16) Which three countries joined NATO in 1999?

17) Why did the UN place sanctions on Iraq in 1990?

18) What was the Oil-for-Food Programme?

19) What was the name of the UN force sent to help rebuild Kosovo?

Russia Under the Tsars

Before the First World War, the Tsar held supreme power in Russia.

The Government of the Russian Empire was Unpopular

Tsar
Nicholas II

Absolute ruler: His dynasty had ruled Russia for 300 years. Increasingly unpopular.

Peasants: 85% of people. Poor people using old, inefficient farming methods.

Industrial workers: Had low wages and poor working conditions. Industry was growing.

1) The Tsar was all-powerful — he ruled <u>without a parliament</u>, and most of the country's wealth and land was owned by a small noble class. The Church taught that the Tsar must be <u>obeyed</u>.

2) Peasant villages were controlled by the <u>mir</u> — a local council who interfered in everyone's business and had the power to <u>decide</u> whether a peasant was <u>allowed</u> to own or rent <u>land</u>.

3) The growth of <u>industry</u> meant there was a large working population in the towns — but conditions in the towns were <u>cramped</u> and the workers were <u>badly paid</u>.

4) In 1905 Russia was <u>defeated</u> in a war with Japan.

5) Poor conditions led to <u>strikes</u> and <u>demonstrations</u> — on 'Bloody Sunday' troops fired into a crowd of peaceful demonstrators in St Petersburg. There was <u>nearly</u> a popular <u>revolution</u>.

The Tsar allowed some Change and set up a Parliament

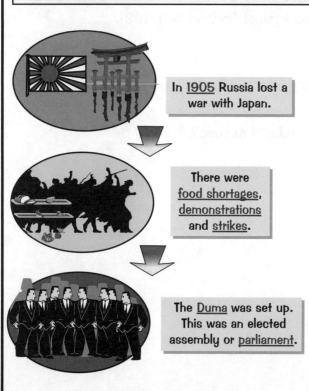

In <u>1905</u> Russia lost a war with Japan.

There were <u>food shortages</u>, <u>demonstrations</u> and <u>strikes</u>.

The <u>Duma</u> was set up. This was an elected assembly or <u>parliament</u>.

1) In the first <u>Duma</u> of 1906, the liberal <u>Constitutional Democratic Party</u> (known as the Cadets) won a majority. They demanded <u>control</u> of <u>taxes</u>, as the Tsar had promised them.

2) Instead he <u>dismissed</u> the Duma and many Liberals <u>fled</u> to Finland. New elections were held.

3) This time the Duma was even more radical — members of the <u>Marxist SDLP</u> (Social Democratic Labour Party — see p.40) <u>won</u> some seats from the Cadets. When the Tsar wanted to <u>arrest</u> several SDLP members as terrorists the Duma <u>refused</u> — so the Tsar <u>dismissed</u> it too.

4) The next two Dumas <u>obeyed</u> the Tsar (1907-1914). The SDLP were not allowed to run as candidates and any known '<u>troublemakers</u>' were arrested and <u>imprisoned</u>.

5) The press was <u>censored</u> and a secret police was used to <u>spy</u> on people the Tsar feared.

6) The situation of the people hadn't improved and there was still a lot of <u>discontent</u> among the <u>poor</u> working classes.

Tsarist Russia — dumb and Duma...

The Tsar had <u>autocratic power</u> in 1914 — that means he had the final say on everything. But as events earlier in the century had shown, there were plenty of people who were prepared to go to great lengths pressing for <u>reform</u>.

Countdown to Revolution

Attempts were made to fix Russia's problems, but World War I made everything more difficult.

Attempted Reform hit Problems — 1906-1911

1) Stolypin became the Prime Minister of Russia in 1906 and wanted economic reforms — he was afraid that badly run industry could get out of control.
2) He ended the control of the mir over how land was distributed. Hard-working peasants could now rent or buy land to farm themselves — helped by special peasant banks. These better-off peasants were known as kulaks.
3) The mir system continued but became less efficient when the kulaks left — causing problems for the country's food supply.
4) Peasants in the mir farms resented the wealth of some kulaks.
5) Reform needed peace, but Europe was heading for war (see section 1).
6) Stolypin was murdered in 1911 by a revolutionary.

Tsar Nicholas' wife was influenced by a 'Holy Man' called Rasputin who claimed supernatural powers to treat the Tsar's son for haemophilia — a disease where the blood won't clot. Rasputin became powerful and even sacked and appointed government ministers. He was killed by angry nobles in 1916 — but the Tsar's authority had been undermined.

Rasputin

The First World War caused more Problems

Patriotism and loyalty to the Tsar were revived. People wanted a short and victorious war, but:

1) There were high casualties — 1 800 000 Russian soldiers dead by the end of 1917.
2) There was a shortage of rifles and equipment. Poor transport slowed supplies to the front.
3) Military leadership was bad — the Tsar took personal command in 1915. This meant he was often away at the Eastern Front — leaving his unpopular wife in charge in the capital.
4) The Russian army was pushed back by the Germans and there was a stalemate.
5) Inflation meant that prices at home went up massively.
6) There was widespread hunger and food and fuel shortages at home.

The 'February' Revolution of 1917

1) Demonstrations and food riots suddenly broke out in the capital city of Petrograd.
2) The Tsar had lost support and control — when his soldiers were ordered to fire on the mobs many refused or deserted to join the rioting workers.
3) The Tsar gave up the throne. A Provisional Government was formed under the leadership of Prince Lvov until July, and then Kerensky. Russia was now a republic.
4) The main revolutionary parties were taken by surprise — this was a real people's revolution caused by sudden risings of workers and soldiers sick of the war, shortages and high prices.
5) This meant that the new government could face opposition from the revolutionaries, who wanted power for themselves — among them, a group from the SDLP called the Bolsheviks.

The end of Tsarism — the people were revolting...

The Russian calendar was behind the Western one at this time — by about two weeks. This means that the 'October' Revolution took place in our November, and the 'February' Revolution in our March. The Bolsheviks changed their calendar to the same system as ours in 1918.

The Bolsheviks

The Bolshevik Party would come to play a huge part in the history of Russia. Here's some background on them and their <u>Marxist</u> beliefs.

Marxism said Capitalism was Wrong

1) Capitalism is the economic system based on <u>business</u> — selling things to make a <u>profit</u>.
2) <u>Marx</u>, a 19th-century political thinker, said this was <u>unjust</u> because thousands of workers were receiving low wages for labour that made a tiny elite class very rich.
3) According to Marx, history is a process of <u>development</u> towards an ideal society — change comes because of <u>class struggle</u> between the middle class and working class.
4) This would in time lead to a <u>violent revolution</u> by the workers. After the revolution, the means of <u>production</u> would be used for everyone's benefit and <u>shared</u> — this is called <u>communism</u>.

The SDLP were the Marxist Party in Russia

In the late 1890s and early 1900s, the SDLP <u>encouraged</u> the industrial workers in the towns to <u>protest</u> against their terrible living conditions. They hoped to <u>create</u> a situation where a <u>Marxist revolution</u> could take place. Many of them were <u>exiled</u> by the Tsarist government — this was one reason they weren't involved in the February Revolution.

The Bolsheviks came out of the SDLP

Lenin

1) At the Social Democrat Conference of 1903, the SDLP <u>quarrelled</u> over whether to become a <u>mass party</u> (open to anyone) or to remain a <u>small party</u> of dedicated members working towards revolution.
2) The party <u>split</u> into <u>Bolsheviks</u> who wanted a small party and were led by <u>Lenin</u>, and <u>Mensheviks</u> led by <u>Martov</u> who wanted a mass party.

Vladimir Ilyich Lenin was the Bolshevik leader. He was a <u>clever thinker</u> and a <u>practical</u> man — he knew how to take advantage of events.

The Bolsheviks were a Small Party

1) At first, the Bolsheviks were <u>too small</u> a party to make much <u>impact</u> on the workers.
2) During the war, Lenin was in <u>exile</u> in Switzerland. When the February Revolution came he returned to Russia to rally the Bolshevik cause.
3) The Germans <u>helped</u> him to return in a sealed train in April 1917, because they <u>hoped</u> he would cause another <u>revolution</u> and that Russia would <u>end</u> the war.

Lenin's 'April Theses' Urged Revolution

1) Lenin issued a document called the <u>April Theses</u>, promising '<u>peace, bread, land and freedom</u>'.
2) He called for an <u>end</u> to the 'capitalist' war, and demanded that <u>power</u> should be given to the <u>Soviets</u> — elected committees of workers, peasants and soldiers which had started up in 1905 and had given <u>leadership</u> to the people during the February Revolution.

Peace + Land + Bread

3) He demanded a revolution <u>against</u> the Provisional Government as soon as possible.

Learn your theory — it's easy Marx...

The Bolsheviks were a <u>revolutionary</u> party. They didn't just want to be the government — they wanted to make <u>big changes</u> to the political system, the economy and society.

The Provisional Government

The situation was <u>very tricky</u> for the Provisional Government.

The Provisional Government had Problems

1) It <u>wasn't</u> supposed to <u>stay</u> in power — but the economic crisis made <u>elections impossible</u>.
2) <u>Inflation</u> grew <u>worse</u>. By November 1917, prices were ten times higher than they were in 1914.
3) Food shortages became worse and peasants began to <u>seize land</u> from noble estates.
4) The new government <u>didn't end</u> the war — soldiers and sailors began to <u>mutiny</u>.
5) A <u>network</u> of <u>Soviets</u> was established — the <u>Petrograd Soviet</u> became an alternative government. Key workers were told to strike to <u>undermine</u> the Provisional Government.
6) The Petrograd Soviet issued <u>'Order No. 1'</u> which said that soldiers shouldn't obey orders from the Provisional Government if they were opposed by the Soviet.

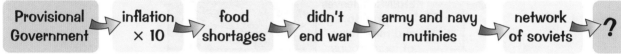

The Soviets demanded an <u>end</u> to the war, but the army <u>attacked</u> the German forces in June 1917. After early Russian success the Germans <u>counter-attacked</u>, forcing a <u>retreat</u> and the <u>collapse</u> of morale and discipline in the Russian army.

The Bolsheviks Prepared for Further Revolution

The Bolsheviks gained <u>increasing support</u> among workers and soldiers with their slogan:

1) In July 1917 the Bolsheviks tried to <u>take control</u> of the government but were <u>defeated</u> and <u>Lenin</u> was forced to leave the country and <u>flee</u> to Finland.

All power to the Soviets

2) Kerensky had turned public opinion against Lenin by <u>accusing</u> him of being a <u>German agent</u>.
3) <u>Leon Trotsky</u> led the <u>Red Guards</u> — a Bolshevik military force. At the same time, the Bolsheviks won control of the Soviets, and Trotsky was <u>chairman</u> of the Petrograd Soviet.
4) Peasants <u>attacked</u> kulaks and <u>took land</u> from the Church and nobles.
5) Many <u>soldiers</u> started to <u>desert</u> from the army and returned home.

General Kornilov attempted a Military Coup

1) In September 1917, the Russian Commander in Chief, General <u>Kornilov</u>, turned his army back from the Front and <u>marched against</u> the Provisional Government determined to seize power.
2) Kerensky had to <u>give weapons</u> to the Bolsheviks and the Petrograd Soviet to <u>save</u> his government from a military takeover.
3) <u>Bolshevik</u> railway workers and <u>Red Guards</u> were waiting to stop Kornilov's advance — but all his soldiers <u>deserted</u> him and he fled.
4) The Bolsheviks were now the <u>real power</u> in Russia, and Lenin <u>encouraged</u> Trotsky to prepare plans for seizing power.

The Bolshevik Press — it was red all over...

The Provisional Government was only supposed to be <u>temporary</u>, which was one of the reasons it was so vulnerable to attempts to <u>overthrow</u> it. Make sure you learn all the <u>events</u> that eventually led to its <u>downfall</u> and remember that the Russian <u>calendar</u> was different to ours, too.

The Bolsheviks Seize Power

The 'October' Revolution of 1917

The <u>Bolshevik Central Committee</u> under Lenin <u>voted</u> for <u>revolution</u>. Detailed plans were made by Trotsky to seize important buildings in Petrograd and arrest ministers. The revolution started on <u>24th October</u> and the Bolsheviks were in control by the next day.

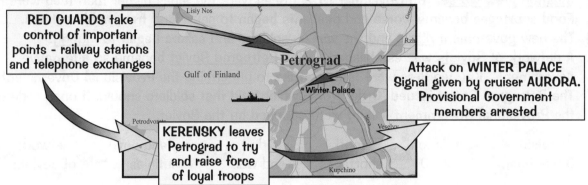

RED GUARDS take control of important points - railway stations and telephone exchanges

KERENSKY leaves Petrograd to try and raise force of loyal troops

Attack on WINTER PALACE Signal given by cruiser AURORA. Provisional Government members arrested

There were only 250 000 Bolsheviks in Russia, controlling a small part of the country — <u>civil war</u> was inevitable as there were <u>many</u> people who were <u>opposed</u> to Bolshevik rule.

Lenin was <u>ruthless</u> and <u>determined</u> to keep power. He knew a strong government was needed — so the ideals of communism had to wait.

The Bolsheviks Established Control

1) The <u>All-Russian Congress of Soviets</u> gave <u>power</u> to the <u>Soviet Council of People's Commissars</u> under Lenin, on 26th October 1917.
2) <u>Soldiers</u> were sent into the countryside to <u>seize grain</u> to feed the towns.
3) The Bolsheviks <u>controlled</u> the main centres of power and used <u>telegraph communications</u> to spread their revolutionary message to local groups.
4) <u>Elections</u> were held for a new constituent assembly. Bolsheviks won 168 seats out of 703, with <u>most seats</u> going to the <u>Socialist Revolutionary Party</u> (SRP), who had peasant support.
5) After one day the Red Guards <u>closed down</u> the Assembly — January 1918.
6) The Bolsheviks became the <u>Communist Party</u>, the only legal party in Russia.
7) Lenin made two decrees (orders) — the <u>Decree on Land</u> nationalised all land in Russia and the <u>Decree on Peace</u> called for peace with Germany.

The Reasons for the Bolshevik Success

1) They were <u>strong</u> in key political and administrative centres — especially <u>Petrograd</u>.
2) They had their <u>own</u> trained <u>military force</u> — the Red Guards.
3) They were ruthless and <u>planned clear strategies</u> — they were prepared for swift action.
4) They were <u>practical</u> — they recognised that the time for a true Marxist revolution was a long way off and so they <u>changed</u> their policies in order to seize power at the first chance. They claimed they ran a <u>socialist government</u> which was trying to create the <u>right conditions</u> for communism in the <u>long term</u> — so in the <u>short term</u> they could do <u>whatever</u> they liked.
5) The continuing problems of war and famine, and the breakdown of law and order, <u>weren't</u> dealt with by the Provisional Government, who had become a <u>weak target</u>.
6) The vision and ability of <u>Lenin</u> — he was a <u>quick-thinking</u> leader who inspired his party.

"Learn it all well" — Lenin's Decree on Revision...

The <u>'October' Revolution</u> was one of those big moments in history when a relatively <u>small group of people</u> have a <u>huge impact</u>. Make sure you learn the reasons why the Bolsheviks were successful.

1918 — Ending the German War

The Bolsheviks took Russia out of one war, and prepared for another one.

The Germans were Advancing

1) The Bolsheviks signed an armistice with the Germans, hoping to delay the peace treaties because they thought there might be a communist revolution in Germany too.

2) This didn't happen, and the German armies advanced — so the Bolsheviks quickly agreed to the harsh terms of the Treaty of Brest-Litovsk in March 1918.

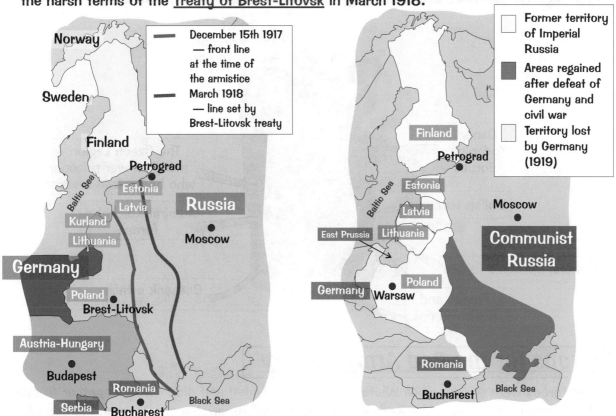

Germany was defeated by the Western allies later in 1918 and some lands were regained.

A Civil War was Inevitable

Lenin and Trotsky were prepared for this. The reasons the civil war broke out were:

1) The communists had seized power suddenly and repressed the elected Constituent Assembly — they had also outlawed political opposition, so many people saw them as a danger.

2) Anti-communist army officers were no longer fighting Germany — many were royalists and wanted the return of the Tsar — and now they could attack the communists.

3) Communists wanted a world revolution — the Comintern (the Communist International) was formed under Zinoviev to promote revolution abroad and to encourage friendly governments in nearby European countries.

The government moved from Petrograd to Moscow in 1918 — Leon Trotsky began to build an efficient Red Army to fight the civil war.

The civil war — not a very polite affair...

Remember — a civil war was the last thing Russia needed after the disasters of the First World War, but the communists knew it was coming, which was why they made peace with Germany at any cost. Scribble down the names of the lands lost by Russia.

The Civil War 1918-1921

The first big challenge for the new Bolshevik government was the brutal civil war.

Anti-Communist forces surrounded Red Russia

1) These armies were called the 'Whites' — the colour of the Tsarist state.
2) There were many White groups who often had different aims and purposes — a key problem.
3) Britain, France and the USA sent troops to help the Whites — trying to restart the Eastern Front against Germany, and worried by communist ideas of world revolution.

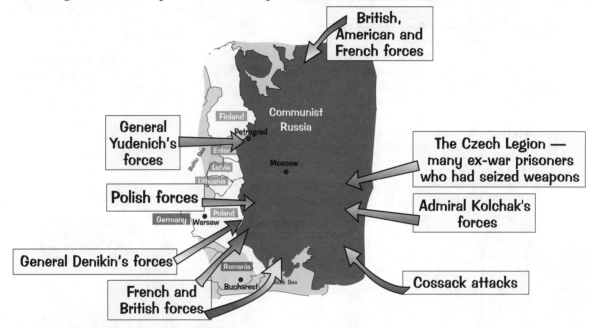

Reasons for the Red Army Victory

1) Red forces were united, while White forces were divided and didn't work together to surround their enemy. This meant the Reds could fight the White armies one by one, instead of fighting on several fronts at the same time. Trotsky was also a brilliant leader.
2) White forces were a long way apart and couldn't stay in touch to coordinate attacks. Some had different political opinions — which meant they didn't want to work together.
3) Patriotic Russians supported the Reds — the Whites were led by nobles and foreign armies.
4) Foreign military support was soon withdrawn as it became clear the Reds would win.
5) The communists controlled the main cities and communications systems — and the railways.
6) The strict and ruthless laws of War Communism helped obtain supplies for the Reds.
7) When the Red Army had defeated its enemies in Russia it carried on and pushed into Poland, hoping to link up with communists in Germany to spread revolution throughout Europe — but it was defeated by the Poles outside Warsaw in late 1920. The war ended with a treaty in 1921.

The Tsar and his Family were Killed

1) The Tsar and his family were held prisoner in a house at Ekaterinburg, because the communists knew they were an important symbol for the White cause.
2) They were executed by the Bolsheviks in 1918 as White forces approached the town.

Success in Europe — the Reds go marching on...

Plenty for you to learn here — looking at the map you'd have thought the Whites would win easily. Focus on the Whites' lack of coordination and the strength of communist control.

War Communism and Mutiny

War Communism — a *Strict System* to *Win* the war

1) Farms and factories were put under <u>state</u> control — private trade was banned.
2) <u>Food was taken</u> for soldiers and industrial workers — peasants who <u>refused</u> to hand it over to the Red Army were shot or sent to <u>forced labour camps</u>.
3) The <u>secret police</u> (Cheka) hunted and executed any <u>enemies</u> of the state.
4) Industrial workers <u>weren't allowed</u> to <u>strike</u> or be absent from work. They could be sent to any region. Experts were brought in to improve efficiency.
5) <u>All adults</u> had to <u>work</u> except for the sick and pregnant women.
6) The results were <u>famine</u> and <u>decline</u>.

Food shortages from 1920 — and famine from 1921 — over 7 million people died of hunger.

Worthless currency abandoned — wages paid in fuel and food.

Workers leave cities, little food in towns. Industry declines.

The Kronstadt *Naval Base* Mutinied

The sailors were <u>unhappy</u> with the lack of progress, the famine and the terror. They <u>mutinied</u> and seized the base near Petrograd, in February 1921.

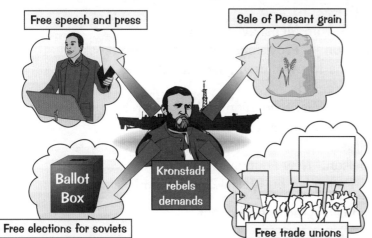

Free speech and press

Sale of Peasant grain

Ballot Box

Kronstadt rebels demands

Free elections for soviets

Free trade unions

1) The Kronstadt sailors had <u>supported</u> the communists in 1917 — especially <u>Trotsky's leadership</u> in Petrograd.
2) Despite this, Lenin and Trotsky were <u>worried</u> that dissent might <u>spread</u> when the ice around the island base <u>thawed</u> and let the sailors leave.
3) Trotsky <u>ordered</u> the Red Army to <u>put down</u> the mutiny.
4) The Red Army <u>attacked</u>, losing many men, but <u>captured</u> it in a brutal battle.
5) Many rebels were <u>killed</u> in the fighting — those who were left were either <u>executed</u> or <u>imprisoned</u> as traitors.

There were other revolts — peasants in Tambov Province <u>robbed</u> food convoys and many factories suffered <u>strikes</u> and <u>unrest</u>.

Lenin *Decided* to *Change* Communist Policy

1) Communism was pushing ahead '<u>too fast</u>' — Trotsky had recognised the economic crisis in 1920 and suggested a <u>change of policy</u> to encourage businesses. Lenin <u>rejected</u> this at first.
2) Now the civil war was won, the communists needed to <u>keep control</u> of public opinion.
3) This meant a policy of <u>complete party unity</u> — no dissent or splits allowed.
4) In 1921 Lenin introduced the <u>New Economic Policy (NEP)</u> to restore <u>order</u> and increase <u>prosperity</u> after the chaos of revolution, civil war and War Communism.

War Communism — not an overwhelming success then...

The Bolsheviks survived in part due to Lenin's willingness to change a <u>failing policy</u>.

The New Economic Policy

The New Economic Policy Reversed War Communism

1) Peasants could <u>sell</u> surplus food produce and pay <u>tax</u> on profits.
2) <u>Small businesses</u>, like shops and small factories, no longer <u>had</u> to be state-owned — the private owners were therefore able to make a profit.
3) Vital <u>industries</u> such as coal, iron, steel, railways, shipping and finance stayed in state hands. But here experts were brought in on <u>higher salaries</u>, and extra wages were paid for <u>efficiency</u>.

The <u>NEP</u> allowed <u>economic recovery</u> — by 1928 industrial and food production levels were about the same as in 1914, and some people grew rich.

Communist political Control Grew

1) A 'purge' in 1921 <u>expelled</u> about a third of party members — those who <u>didn't agree</u> with Lenin.
2) Communist governments were <u>imposed</u> in areas <u>recaptured</u> in the civil war, against the will of independent nationalists such as in the <u>Ukraine</u>.
3) A <u>new constitution</u> established the <u>USSR</u> — Union of Soviet Socialist Republics.
4) Each Republic had a government with some policy freedom, but they all <u>had</u> to be communist, and the system was run centrally by the <u>Politburo</u> — the senior council.

Lenin Died on Jan 21, 1924

1870	Lenin born.
1898	First Congress of the SDLP.
1903	Bolsheviks (majority) split from Mensheviks (minority).
1917	February — First Revolution — Provisional Government (Kerensky).
	April — Lenin outlines plans to overthrow government.
	July — Bolshevik rising defeated.
	October — Bolshevik communist revolution and takeover.
1918	March — Peace treaty with Germany (Brest-Litovsk)
1918-21	Civil war. Reds vs Whites.
1921	Famine. Kronstadt rebellion. New Economic Policy.
1922	Lenin ill after a stroke. Policy led by Stalin, Zinoviev and Kamenev.

Lenin died in 1924. Petrograd was renamed Leningrad in his honour.

Lenin's Key Strengths as a Leader

1) His <u>organisation</u> and <u>leadership</u> of the Bolshevik party transformed it.
2) He had a <u>pragmatic</u> and <u>realistic</u> approach to problems.
3) He was able to <u>'seize the moment'</u>, which was vital in the Bolsheviks gaining power.
4) He could be <u>ruthless</u> — he set up the Cheka (secret police) and the labour camps. He also wasn't afraid to use force to put down the Kronstadt mutiny.
5) He was able to <u>change</u> his <u>policies</u> — e.g. he was able to adopt War Communism to win the civil war, and then to introduce the NEP afterwards to help the economy recover.

<u>Trotsky</u> too played a huge part in the revolution. He was a great <u>theorist</u> and <u>speaker</u> — much of the tactical planning for the Bolshevik seizure of power was his. He also put together the <u>Red Army</u> that won the Civil War. And he was prepared to be <u>brutal</u>, as in the crushing of the Kronstadt mutiny (see p.45).

The New Economic Policy — so new it wasn't even communist...

The NEP <u>reversed</u> War Communism. Scribble a list of the big <u>differences</u> between the two policies.

Revision Summary

And now it's time for your favourite part of every section — those sublime revision questions.
I bet you can't wait.

1) Who beat Russia in a war in 1905?
2) What was the Duma?
3) Who was the Prime Minister of Russia from 1906 to 1911?
4) Who was Rasputin?
5) Explain the impact that the First World War had on Russia.
6) When did the Tsar give up the throne?
7) Why was Kerensky's government 'Provisional'?
8) What were the main beliefs of Marxism?
9) Why were communists split into Bolsheviks and Mensheviks?
10) What did the 'April Theses' promise?
11) Give three problems the Provisional Government faced.
12) What was the Petrograd Soviet's 'Order Number 1'?
13) Which General marched against the Provisional Government in September 1917?
14) How did the Bolsheviks seize power in 1917?
15) What are the names of the two decrees Lenin made right after the revolution?
16) Give four reasons for the Bolsheviks' success.
17) Why were the Bolsheviks prepared to agree to the Brest-Litovsk Treaty?
18) Give two reasons why civil war broke out in Russia in 1918.
19) Consider the events of the civil war — why did the 'Reds' win and the 'Whites' lose?
20) What happened to the Russian royal family in 1918?
21) What were the main elements of War Communism?
22) What were the results of the civil war on the economy, farming and industry?
23) What was the Kronstadt rebellion and how was it dealt with?
24) Write down the main features of the New Economic Policy, and its results.
25) When did Lenin die?
26) Write a short summary of Lenin's achievements.

The Weimar Republic

Germany <u>lost</u> the First World War (1914-1918). The peace settlement was <u>harsh</u> on Germany — it said Germany should accept blame for the war and pay £6.6 billion reparations.

A New Government took over when the Kaiser Abdicated

1) <u>Kaiser Wilhelm II</u> had ruled the German Empire as a <u>monarch</u>. At the end of the First World War there was a period of <u>violent unrest</u> in Germany — and the Kaiser was forced to abdicate in November 1918.

2) In early 1919, a <u>new government</u> took power led by <u>Friedrich Ebert</u> — it changed Germany into a <u>republic</u>. It was set up in <u>Weimar</u>, because there was violence in Berlin. <u>Ebert</u> became the first President, with <u>Scheidemann</u> as Chancellor.

3) Ebert was leader of the <u>Social Democratic Party</u>, a moderate party of socialists. The new government was <u>democratic</u> — they believed the people should say how the country was run.

4) The new German government <u>wasn't invited</u> to the peace conference in 1919 — and had <u>no say</u> in the <u>Versailles Treaty</u>. At first, Ebert <u>refused</u> to sign the treaty, but in the end he had little choice — Germany was too <u>weak</u> to risk restarting the conflict.

The Weimar Constitution made Germany a Republic

THE WEIMAR GOVERNMENT

REICHSRAT
(Upper house — could delay measures passed by Reichstag).

REICHSTAG
The new German parliament (elected by proportional representation).

PRESIDENT
Elected every 7 years. Head of army. Chooses the Chancellor.

Friedrich Ebert

<u>Proportional representation</u> is where the number of <u>seats</u> a party wins in parliament is worked out as a <u>proportion</u> of the number of <u>votes</u> they win. This was the system in Germany and it often led to <u>lots</u> of political parties in the Reichstag (German parliament) — making it <u>harder</u> to get laws passed.

The Weimar Republic had many Problems

1) It was <u>difficult</u> to make decisions because there were so <u>many parties</u> in the Reichstag.

2) It was hard to pick a Chancellor who had the <u>support</u> of most of the Reichstag.

3) The new government had to <u>accept</u> the Versailles Treaty, so they were <u>hated</u> by many Germans because of the loss of territory, the 'war guilt' clause, the reparations etc. (see p.8).

4) Some Germans joined paramilitary groups, such as the <u>Freikorps</u> (Free Corps) — <u>right-wing</u> groups made up of <u>ex-soldiers</u> who saw <u>communists</u> as a threat to <u>peace</u>.

5) Even though the <u>Freikorps</u> were problematic — they were <u>private organisations</u> not under government <u>control</u> — Ebert was happy to use them to <u>suppress</u> communist uprisings.

Weimar — not a kind of sausage...

The <u>Weimar Republic</u> was set up in a time of <u>defeat</u> — which made it unpopular right from the start. Don't forget — many German people <u>didn't accept</u> the peace settlement at the end of the First World War. Scribble a quick paragraph on the Weimar Republic and how it was set up.

The Years of Unrest

Germany faced all sorts of <u>problems</u> in the years following the First World War.

Reasons _for_ Discontent

1) Thousands of people were <u>poor</u> and <u>starving</u>. An <u>influenza</u> epidemic had killed thousands.
2) Many Germans <u>denied</u> they had lost the war and blamed the <u>'November Criminals'</u> who had agreed to the Armistice and the Treaty of Versailles.
3) Others <u>blamed</u> for losing the war included the communists, the government and the Jews.
4) The government was seen as <u>weak</u> and <u>ineffective</u> — the <u>Treaty of Versailles</u> had made living conditions <u>worse</u> in Germany.

Soon there were Riots and Rebellions

1) In 1919, the <u>communists,</u> led by Karl Liebknecht and Rosa Luxemburg, tried to <u>take over</u> Berlin in the <u>Spartacist Revolt</u> — but they were defeated by the Freikorps.

Wolfgang Kapp

2) In 1920, some of the right-wing Freikorps themselves took part in the Kapp Putsch (Putsch means revolt). Led by Wolfgang Kapp, they <u>took over</u> Berlin to form another government. The workers staged a General Strike — Kapp <u>gave up</u>. The government <u>didn't</u> punish the rebels, because many judges <u>sympathised</u> with people like Kapp.

3) In 1922 Walter Rathenau was <u>killed</u> — he'd been the Foreign Minister who <u>signed</u> the Rapallo Treaty with Russia and was <u>Jewish</u>. Many Germans were now anti-Jewish (<u>anti-Semitic</u>).

In 1923 Germany Couldn't Pay _the_ Reparations

France and Belgium occupied the Ruhr — the <u>richest</u> industrial part of Germany — to <u>take resources</u> instead. This led to fury in Germany, while workers in the Ruhr <u>refused</u> to work. German industry was devastated again, plunging the economy into <u>hyperinflation</u>.

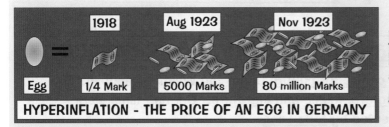

	1918	Aug 1923	Nov 1923
Egg	1/4 Mark	5000 Marks	80 million Marks

HYPERINFLATION - THE PRICE OF AN EGG IN GERMANY

<u>Hyperinflation</u> happens when production can't keep up with the amount of money there is, so the <u>money</u> keeps <u>losing its value</u>.

Hyperinflation had Three Major Results

1) <u>Wages</u> were paid <u>twice a day</u> before prices went up again.
2) The middle classes lost out as <u>bank savings</u> became <u>worthless</u>.
3) The German <u>Mark</u> became <u>worthless</u>.

Hyperinflation — sounds good for blowing up balloons...

Remember that discontent in Germany got <u>worse</u> when the economy <u>went wrong</u> — but there were lots of other factors too. Scribble a list of <u>reasons</u> why there was so much discontent.

Stresemann and Recovery

In August 1923 Stresemann became Chancellor — he gradually led Germany back to recovery.

Stresemann wanted International Cooperation

Stresemann was Chancellor for a few months, then Foreign Minister. He believed Germany's best chance for recovery came from working with other countries.

1) In September 1923 he told the workers in the Ruhr to return to work.

2) He accepted the Dawes Plan in 1924, and introduced a new German Mark called the Rentenmark to make the currency more stable.

3) In 1925 the French and Belgian troops left the Ruhr.

4) In October 1925 he agreed to the Locarno Treaty where the western borders of Germany were agreed, but not the eastern. He won the Nobel Peace Prize for his efforts in this field.

5) In 1926, Germany joined the League of Nations, and became one of the permanent members of the Council.

6) In 1928, Germany was one of 65 countries to sign the Kellogg-Briand Pact. They promised not to use violence to settle disputes.

7) In 1929, the Young Plan replaced the Dawes Plan — reparations would be reduced by three-quarters of the amount, and Germany was given 59 years to pay them.

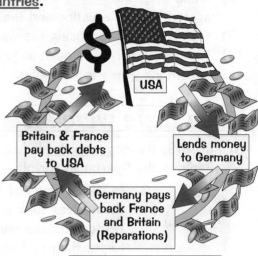

USA

Britain & France pay back debts to USA

Lends money to Germany

Germany pays back France and Britain (Reparations)

The Dawes Plan

Germany had begun to Recover — but Depended on US Money

Gustav Stresemann

Life was beginning to look better for Germany thanks to the work of Stresemann. But he died in October 1929, just before the disaster of the Wall Street Crash (see p.11). The plans he had agreed would only work if the USA had enough money to keep lending to Germany — but now it didn't. Things were suddenly going to get worse again.

The Weimar Republic had many Cultural Achievements

1) Germany's capital Berlin became a centre for culture under the Weimar Republic.

2) There were advances in art, architecture, music and literature. German films were successful — e.g. 'Metropolis', directed by Fritz Lang.

3) Some developments were bold and new, like the drama of Bertolt Brecht. The Bauhaus School of design was highly influential.

4) The Weimar Republic encouraged new ways of critical thinking at places like Frankfurt University.

5) Not everyone approved of these cultural changes — the cabaret culture in Berlin was seen as immoral by some. The culture of the Weimar Republic didn't survive under the Nazis...

It was nearly all okay...

The 1920s were a tough decade in Germany, but Stresemann seemed to have the problems sorted. Scribble a paragraph on the work of Stresemann — his policies at home and abroad.

The Roots of the Nazi Party

The <u>Nazi Party</u> was a small organisation in the 1920s — but it had big ambitions...

Adolf Hitler was the Nazi Leader

1) Born in Austria in <u>1889</u>, Hitler had lived in Germany from 1912 onwards.
2) He'd been a brave <u>soldier</u> on the Western Front in World War I, winning the Iron Cross twice. He <u>couldn't accept</u> that Germany had <u>lost</u> the war.
3) In 1919, he joined the German Workers' Party, led by <u>Anton Drexler</u>. It was a tiny party — Hitler was the 55th member. In 1920 the name was changed to the <u>National Socialist German Workers' Party</u> (Nazis).
4) Hitler was a <u>charismatic speaker</u> and attracted new members. He took over the <u>leadership</u> of the party.
5) The party set up its own <u>armed group</u> called the <u>Sturmabteilung</u> (<u>SA</u>) — brown-shirted stormtroopers who protected Nazi leaders and <u>harassed</u> their opponents.

Hitler tried to Overthrow the Government in the Munich Putsch

1) In 1923, things were going badly for the Weimar Republic — it seemed <u>weak</u>.
2) Hitler planned to <u>overthrow</u> the <u>Weimar government</u> — starting by taking control of the government in a region called Bavaria.
3) Hitler's soldiers occupied a <u>beer hall</u> in the Bavarian city of <u>Munich</u> where local government leaders were meeting. He announced that the <u>revolution</u> had begun.
4) The next day Hitler marched into Munich supported by stormtroopers. But the revolt quickly <u>collapsed</u> when <u>police</u> fired on the rebels.

Hitler wrote the book 'Mein Kampf' in Prison

1) Hitler was <u>imprisoned</u> for his role in the Munich Putsch.
2) He wrote a book in prison describing his <u>beliefs</u> and <u>ambitions</u>. The title 'Mein Kampf' means 'My Struggle'.

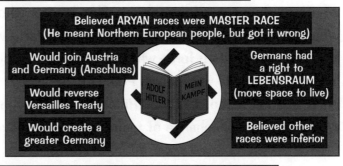

Believed ARYAN races were MASTER RACE
(He meant Northern European people, but got it wrong)

Would join Austria and Germany (Anschluss)

Would reverse Versailles Treaty

Would create a greater Germany

ADOLF HITLER MEIN KAMPF

Germans had a right to LEBENSRAUM (more space to live)

Believed other races were inferior

After the Munich Putsch Hitler Changed Tactics

1) The Nazi party was <u>banned</u> after the Munich Putsch. After Hitler was released from prison, he <u>re-established</u> the party with himself as <u>supreme leader</u>.
2) By the <u>mid-1920s</u>, the German economy was starting to <u>recover</u> under <u>Stresemann</u>. As a result, general support for the Nazis declined and overturning the government through a coup <u>no longer</u> seemed <u>realistic</u>.
3) Hitler <u>changed tactics</u> — he now tried to gain control through the democratic system. The Nazi party network was extended <u>nationally</u>, instead of it being a regional party. <u>Propaganda</u> was used to promote the party's beliefs.

The Nazis — ready to sweep to power...

Very few people supported the Nazis at this stage. There were <u>fewer than 30 000</u> members by 1925, and in the 1928 elections the Nazis had 12 Reichstag members, compared with 54 Communists and 153 Social Democrats. All that was about to <u>change</u> though (see section 11).

Revision Summary

Phew — it's question time again. Now's your chance to show off what you've learned — and to find out what you still need to practise. Weimar Germany is a tricky subject — make sure you know about the long-term consequences of the Versailles Treaty, and the reasons for the weakness of the Weimar government. Remember — it doesn't matter if you can't answer all the questions first time. Go over the section again and keep trying, until you can answer every one. And there's no point in cheating — that won't help you in the exams. So let's get going.

1) What was the name of the first President of the Weimar Republic? Which party did he belong to?

2) Why was the government based at Weimar?

3) What was the name of the parliament in the Weimar Republic?

4) What is the name for the system that used a party's share of the vote in an election to work out the number of seats it got in the Reichstag?

5) Name the force which was started to keep the peace in Germany.

6) Give three reasons for discontent in Germany after World War I.

7) Where did the Spartacist Revolt and the Kapp Putsch take place?

8) Who were the leaders of the Spartacist Revolt?

9) Give the main results of the French occupation of the Ruhr in 1923.

10) Does hyperinflation increase or reduce the value of money?

11) Why did hyperinflation badly hit the middle classes in particular?

12) Write a paragraph outlining the work of Gustav Stresemann.

13) What was the name of the new currency introduced by Stresemann?

14) What did the countries who signed the Kellogg-Briand pact promise?

15) What was the name of the German film director who made 'Metropolis'?

16) Who was the leader of the German Workers' Party when Hitler joined?

17) Name the paramilitary force which was set up to support the Nazis.

18) In which region did the Munich Putsch take place?

19) What was the title of the book Hitler wrote in prison?

20) What was the main change of tactics for the Nazis after the Munich Putsch?

The USA's Reaction to World War One

After the First World War (1914-1918), the USA chose not to get involved in international affairs. This policy was known as isolationism.

The League was the idea of the American President

Woodrow Wilson

1) The League of Nations was largely the idea of the American President Woodrow Wilson. It was one of his Fourteen Points (see p.6) — fourteen principles on which he thought a peace settlement could be based.
2) He thought a League of Nations could act like a world parliament where the representatives of all the major powers would meet to discuss matters of international importance.
3) He was sure that such an organisation could prevent another world war.

But America Never Joined the League of Nations

1) A League of Nations was set up following the end of the First World War, as part of the Treaty of Versailles.
2) Wilson wanted the USA to join the League of Nations, but he needed the approval of the US Congress.
3) The problem was that most Americans didn't want to join.
4) The majority of the American people favoured 'isolationism' — they wanted the USA to remain isolated from foreign entanglements.

Americans Didn't Trust the League of Nations

1) Many Americans had been against the USA getting involved in the First World War and were upset by the loss of American lives.
2) They were worried that if America joined the League of Nations they would be obliged to interfere in conflicts that most Americans thought were none of their business.
3) The USA had a lot of citizens who were German or Austrian immigrants. These people saw the League as linked to the hated Treaty of Versailles (see p.7). They were opposed to the USA joining an organisation that was forcing Germany to pay vast amounts in reparations (damages for the war).
4) Some Americans were suspicious of the French and the British. They were sure that the League would come under British and French control and that America would be called upon to help these countries defend their colonies. Many Americans felt that colonies didn't fit in with their ideas about freedom and democracy and should not be supported.
5) Other Americans were concerned that joining the League of Nations could cost them money. They were worried that the League would drag America into lots of expensive wars. Many businessmen contended that the US had grown prosperous by staying out of European affairs and that it should remain isolated from Europe.

The USA thought it was better off alone...

Perhaps it was a bit selfish of the USA to reject the League of Nations, but they probably did save themselves a lot of trouble and expense, at least in the short-term. Make sure you learn all the reasons for their decision not to join.

Growth of Isolationism

America just wanted to be <u>alone</u>.

The USA Entered Late and Gained From World War One

1) The American economy <u>boomed</u> as a result of the First World War.
2) The USA exported <u>weapons</u> and <u>food</u> to Europe during the war.
3) The USA <u>joined</u> the Allied side in <u>1917</u> — but no fighting happened on American soil.
4) After the war, European countries whose industries had been damaged <u>bought American goods</u> with the help of <u>American loans</u>.

Cheap European Imports were seen as a Threat

1) American <u>businesses</u> were afraid that the USA would be flooded with <u>cheap European imports</u>.
2) <u>Unemployment</u> was higher in <u>Europe</u> so European workers were willing to work for <u>lower wages</u>. Businessmen were worried American consumers would start <u>buying European products</u> rather than the <u>more expensive</u> American ones.
   This would mean: • The <u>loss</u> of American <u>jobs</u>.
   • <u>Lower profits</u> for US companies.
   • Less money in <u>taxes</u> for the US government.

Warren G Harding raised Tariffs to protect US Industry

President Harding

1) Harding was elected President in 1921. He brought in the <u>Emergency Tariff Act</u> of <u>May 1921</u>. A tariff is a <u>tax</u> on imported and exported goods. The act <u>increased</u> the tariff rates on <u>imported farm products</u>.
2) In 1922, the <u>Fordney-McCumber Tariff</u> gave the President the power to raise and lower the tariff rates.
3) Harding used the Fordney-McCumber Tariff to <u>raise duties</u> on both <u>factory</u> and <u>farm</u> goods.
4) He hoped to <u>protect</u> America from "<u>unfair</u>" European competition.

Immigration Control was increased

Before the First World War, America had followed an '<u>Open Door</u>' policy that allowed almost <u>anybody</u> to move to the USA. But some Americans started <u>demanding</u> that this 'door' be <u>closed</u>. The most <u>powerful</u> and <u>wealthy</u> cultural group in America at this time were people with mainly British ancestors — later known as the <u>White Anglo-Saxon Protestants</u> (WASPs).

1) Many WASPs believed that people such as <u>anarchists</u> and <u>communists</u> were coming into the USA and <u>undermining</u> the American way of life.
2) They were also alarmed at the number of <u>Asian</u>, <u>Catholic</u> and <u>Jewish</u> people who were entering the USA.

The WASPs had great influence in <u>Congress</u> (the American parliament).
As a consequence, President Harding decided to place <u>strict limitations on immigration</u>, especially from <u>Eastern</u> and <u>Southern</u> Europe.
In <u>1921</u>, Congress passed an act which introduced a <u>quota system</u>.
Annual immigration was reduced from over one million to about 150 000 in 1929.

Isolationism — it's tariffic...

After the First World War, Europe had lots of <u>problems</u>, while America had <u>relatively few</u>.
By <u>limiting imports</u> and <u>reducing immigration</u>, the US sought to secure its peace and prosperity.

Prosperity in the 1920s

The 1920s were a time of huge economic growth in the US.

The 1920s were a Time of Plenty

This decade was a 'boom time' for many — incomes rose and standards of living improved.

1) There was low inflation, low unemployment and low interest rates.

2) Cities were rebuilt with tall skyscrapers, and major road building programmes were undertaken.

3) There was a consumer boom. More people could now afford items such as radios, refrigerators, washing machines, vacuum cleaners and telephones.

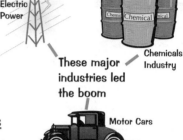

Electric Power

Chemicals Industry

These major industries led the boom

Motor Cars

4) Advertising encouraged more spending and became a big business in itself, expanding into radio and film commercials.

5) Hire purchase (buying in instalments) was introduced to make cars affordable to average earners who could only buy them on credit. It encouraged more spending on luxury goods.

6) Republican government policy contributed to prosperity. The reduction of income tax left people with more money to spend. The government also promoted cheap credit through the Federal Reserve Board (central banking system). They encouraged banks to lend money on easier terms, which (in the short-term) contributed to the boom.

The Stock Market boomed

1.5 million Americans bought shares in the 1920s. Before the price of shares began to rocket unrealistically in 1928, there were sensible reasons for buying them — people were investing in a real boom in production and consumption. It only started to go bad when people took to buying shares on credit in the hope of selling them at a profit (see p.60).

The Motor Industry led the way

1) The jobs of 1 in 12 workers were linked to motorcar production.

2) Car production boosted other industries — steel, petrol, chemicals, glass and rubber.

3) Cars became more affordable — the Model T Ford cost less than $300.

4) Production of cars became dominated by the big three companies — Ford, Chrysler and General Motors.

5) Ford's factory used an assembly line system. It divided manufacturing tasks among a group of workers spaced alongside a moving belt. It made production far more efficient, which allowed for a huge reduction in price. By 1929, there was one car for every five Americans.

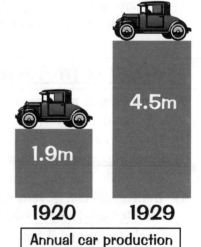

4.5m

1.9m

1920   1929

Annual car production

Boom in the US — revise this and prosper...

This page is really important. It shows you how the American economy really took off in the 1920s. Make sure you learn some of these statistics — they'll impress the examiners.

Poverty in the 1920s

While there was a boom for many Americans, for others life remained a struggle.

There was still Poverty

Wealth wasn't distributed evenly — there was a big gap between rich and poor in the USA.

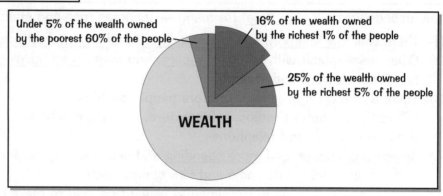

Under 5% of the wealth owned by the poorest 60% of the people

16% of the wealth owned by the richest 1% of the people

25% of the wealth owned by the richest 5% of the people

WEALTH

Some poverty was in Urban Areas

1) Monopolies (where a whole industry is owned or controlled by one company or alliance) kept prices high and wages low, by stopping competition for customers and workers.
2) Many African Americans had moved from the South to the northern states to work in war industries. They were often restricted by prejudice and poverty to living in poor districts.
3) Some urban poverty was produced by the pressure of numbers — many people moved to cities because of rural hardship.

"Old" industries Suffered

1) The coal industry did badly. Coal mining suffered from competition with oil. Cars and trucks began to take over from the railways, which were a major user of coal.
2) About 10% less coal was mined in 1929 than in 1919. More efficient mining technology also caused workers to be laid off, and those that remained saw their wages decrease. The mining towns suffered acute hardship.
3) In 1920 the wartime cotton boom collapsed. In 1921 the boll weevil — a beetle that feeds off cotton plants — destroyed 30% of the crop. In the mid 1920s the opposite problem, overproduction, caused prices to plunge.

Problems in Agriculture led to Rural Poverty

1) Farmers had prospered during the war. But during the 1920s, they grew more food than was needed. Overproduction led to falling prices and so to falling profits.
2) Taxes, mortgages and wages were rising, further reducing farmers' profits.
3) Foreign competition increased during the 1920s. European agriculture recovered from the war, while Canada, Russia, Argentina and Australia also competed on the world market.
4) The Republican government didn't believe in direct help to farmers. When Congress passed the McNary-Haugen bill, to allow the government to buy up farmers' crops, President Coolidge vetoed it twice — he thought it would encourage more overproduction.
5) For the first time ever, the American farm population began to shrink.

The Jazz Age wasn't all Bentleys and champagne...

There are always winners and losers — the 1920s were no different. It's important to remember that some people struggled through what are often thought of as the 'good times'.

Intolerance in the 1920s

Some groups in 1920s America suffered discrimination and persecution.

Prejudice against Immigrants led to the Red Scare

1) There was prejudice against newer immigrant groups and worries about communist agitators entering the country. In 1919 the authorities used a series of bombings across the country to whip up a 'Red Scare'. They deported over 4000 people, mainly Russians.

2) During the Red Scare, two Italian anarchists called Nicola Sacco and Bartolomeo Vanzetti were convicted of murder and robbery. There were protests by people who argued it was a miscarriage of justice, and that the judge was prejudiced. But they were executed in 1927.

- From 1917 immigrants had to pass a 'literacy test' to enter.
- A quota system was introduced in 1921. This was replaced in 1924 by the National Origins Act which strictly limited immigration. This act discriminated against immigrants from Southern and Eastern Europe, and Asia.

The racist Ku Klux Klan (KKK) Expanded

1) First formed in the 1860s, the Ku Klux Klan gained new popularity in the early 1920s.

2) The KKK was a white supremacist organisation based in the southern states of the USA.

3) They opposed African Americans being given more rights. They were also prejudiced against immigrants, Jewish people and Catholics. They used intimidation and violence.

4) KKK membership had grown to around 4 million by 1925.

5) In 1925, there was a scandal involving Indiana KKK leader D.C. Stephenson (he was convicted of kidnapping and second degree murder). The organisation lost much support, and never regained such significant cultural and political power.

Some Laws were Racist

> **DRINKING FOUNTAIN**
> **WHITE ONLY**

1) The 'Jim Crow Laws' was a collective name for laws that discriminated against African Americans. These were more common in the southern states of the USA.

2) Some laws made it difficult for African Americans to vote. For example, it was law in some states that voters had to show that their grandfathers had voted — this excluded many African Americans whose ancestors were slaves with no voting rights (slavery was only abolished in America in 1865).

3) Some laws forced white and African American people to use separate facilities, e.g. different schools, transport, parks, cafes and theatres. This was called segregation. Although the facilities were supposed to be 'separate but equal', the ones provided for African Americans were usually much worse.

There was an ugly, violent side to American society...

Remember — there were many groups who were discriminated against in 1920s USA. It would need decades of protests before African Americans would get their civil rights (see section 13).

Prohibition and Organised Crime

In <u>January 1920</u> it became illegal to manufacture, distribute or sell alcohol. This was <u>Prohibition</u>.

In 1920 America tried to turn *Teetotal*

1) <u>Pressure</u> for Prohibition had built up over a <u>long time</u>. Some states were '<u>dry</u>' by 1917.
2) <u>Temperance movements</u> had been <u>campaigning</u> for Prohibition since the 19th century — they were popular in <u>rural areas</u>, and were often <u>Christian</u>. They claimed alcohol led to <u>violence</u>, <u>immoral behaviour</u>, and the <u>breakdown</u> of family life.
3) The <u>middle class</u> often blamed alcohol for <u>disorder</u> among immigrants and the working class. <u>Businessmen</u> blamed alcohol for making workers <u>unreliable</u>.
4) The First World War (which the USA joined in 1917) resulted in more support for Prohibition. Many breweries were owned by <u>German immigrants</u> — and the USA was fighting Germany.
5) <u>Opposition</u> to <u>Prohibition</u> was mainly in <u>urban</u> areas — especially cities in the northern states.

<u>Saloons</u> were closed down. Buying alcohol illegally was <u>expensive</u>, which caused <u>consumption to decrease</u> — especially among the poor. The US authorities recruited over 1500 <u>agents</u> (later increased to 2800+) to enforce the law.

Organised Crime 'took over' the distribution of alcohol

Prohibition Crime

Hijackers:
Stole smuggled alcohol

Bootleggers:
Sold on redistilled industrial alcohol

Speakeasies:
Illegal drinking clubs sprang up with secret passwords at the door

<u>Millions of dollars</u> were made trading in illegal alcohol. Prohibition saw a massive rise in organised crime as <u>rival gangs</u> fought for control of the business.

Moonshiners:
Made their own liquor

Rum-runners:
Smuggled alcohol from Europe, the West Indies, Canada and Mexico

In Chicago 1926-29, <u>gang warfare</u> led to almost <u>1300 murders</u>. <u>Al Capone</u> was a gang leader:

Al Capone worked for Johnny Torrio, a leading Chicago Gangster.

Taking over from Torrio in 1925, the ruthless Capone was making $60m a year from alcohol and $45m from gambling, dance halls and race tracks.

He used a private army to intimidate voters and fight rival gangs. In 1929, 7 members of a rival gang were machine-gunned in the St Valentine's Day Massacre.

Capone was sentenced to 11 years in prison for tax evasion in 1931. In poor health, he retired to his Florida mansion and died in 1947.

Prohibition finally ended in 1933

Enforcing Prohibition proved impossible. There was <u>public demand</u> for alcohol. Many people were willing to <u>break the law</u> — especially in the <u>cities</u>. Also Prohibition led to <u>corruption</u> — some policemen and judges took <u>bribes</u> or became involved in the liquor trade themselves.

Prohibition — a tee-total disaster...

Prohibition failed because <u>demand</u> for alcohol continued. Criminals quickly moved in to supply people with <u>illegal liquor</u>, making huge profits and developing sophisticated <u>criminal networks</u>.

Social Developments

American society underwent <u>big changes</u> in the 1920s.

Many people had More Money to spend on Leisure

Paperback books

Motor transport

Films

Radio

Jazz music clubs

New dances like the Charleston and Lindy hop

1) <u>Film</u> became the essential <u>mass entertainment</u> — and a multi-million dollar industry. Huge <u>cinemas</u> were built which could seat up to 4000 people. Films were silent until <u>1927</u>, when the first <u>'talking' picture</u> was released. <u>Hollywood</u> was the major film-making centre.

2) <u>Radio</u> also boomed. In 1921 there was just one <u>licensed station</u>. Two years later there were <u>508</u>. Millions of <u>sets</u> were sold. By 1929, $850m was spent on sets and parts every year. The <u>NBC</u> (National Broadcasting Company) was set up in 1926. By 1929 it had made $150m from <u>advertising</u>.

There were changing Manners and Morals

1) Young people enjoyed <u>smoking</u>, <u>dancing</u> and <u>cocktail parties</u>. Some women started to wear <u>lipstick</u>, <u>shorter skirts</u> and <u>high heels</u> (these women were called <u>flappers</u>).
2) Church attendance <u>fell</u> and the divorce rate <u>increased</u>.
3) But many people felt that permissiveness and <u>sexual freedom</u> had gone <u>too far</u>.

Women gained more Freedom and Independence

1) Films, popular songs and paperbacks encouraged <u>new fashions and freedom</u>.
2) Some <u>feminists</u> encouraged liberation, but had only limited success.
3) Women were encouraged to gain <u>economic independence</u> — some learned a trade or trained as typists or secretaries. New <u>office jobs</u> provided employment for many women.
4) Household <u>gadgets</u> gave some relief from <u>domestic drudgery</u>.
5) Rising high school and college attendance meant women were <u>better educated</u> than before.

But Traditional Views continued

1) Some books and magazines tried to set '<u>decent</u>' standards.
2) Women were still expected to be <u>homemakers</u>.
3) In employment there was continuing <u>discrimination against women</u>.
4) The vast majority of working class women continued in <u>low-skilled, low-paid jobs</u>.
5) Traditional male values continued to emphasise the <u>superiority of men</u> in the 'public sphere'.

Hollywood, short skirts — and all that jazz...

What a great couple of pages to learn here — <u>gangsters</u>, <u>flappers</u>, <u>film stars</u>, they're all here. Don't get carried away though — you still need to know all these facts in detail for the exam.

The Wall Street Crash

Wall Street is the <u>major financial centre</u> in New York. Stocks and shares are bought and sold there.

On Black Thursday share prices Plummeted

On Thursday 24th October 1929 around 13 million shares were sold. <u>Confidence</u> in the value of <u>shares</u> began to fall. On 28th and 29th October, a series of sharp falls began in the value of shares.

- Some major stocks lost <u>three quarters</u> of their value.
- Prices continued to <u>fall for years</u>.
- At the lowest point in 1933, 83% of the stock market's value had been lost.

Efforts to Shore Up prices Failed

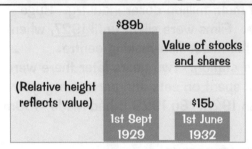

Value of stocks and shares

(Relative height reflects value)

$89b — 1st Sept 1929
$15b — 1st June 1932

Most early losers were <u>large-scale speculators</u>. Leading financiers met to pool <u>$240m</u>. They used this to <u>buy shares</u> in an attempt to <u>restore confidence</u> and <u>stop panic</u>.

They failed — <u>panic selling</u> led to further falls.
- Investment trusts were unable to meet their obligations.
- <u>Defaulting</u> on debts led to bankruptcy for others.
- People rushed to withdraw their savings from <u>banks</u>, causing many banks to go bust.

Underlying Economic Problems contributed to the Crash

Though the 1920s had been a 'boom time' for many, there were <u>serious problems</u> with the economy. Prosperity depended on <u>people continuing to spend</u>. But many people had run up <u>large debts</u>, or had already bought the consumer goods they needed. After 1927 there was a <u>downturn</u> in demand.

This situation was <u>made even worse</u> for a number of reasons.

1) <u>Wealth was distributed unevenly</u> — rising profits were not passed on to workers, so most people were too poor to spend more. This meant demand did not rise as fast as production.
2) There was <u>overproduction</u> — industry was producing more than people wanted to buy. By 1929, unsold stock was building up and manufacturers reduced production. They started to lay off staff and <u>unemployment</u> increased.
3) <u>Banks were largely unregulated</u>. They were unstable and gambled depositors' money on the stock exchange.
4) Brokers provided <u>expensive loans</u> to enable investors to <u>buy shares</u>. When the stock market crashed, investors could not pay back their loans.
5) There were <u>barriers to trade</u> (such as high tariffs) between the USA and Europe — partly because of the USA's policy of <u>isolationism</u> (see p.54). Plus European countries had <u>suffered economically</u> because of the First World War. This meant Europe <u>couldn't</u> provide a <u>good market</u> for America's surplus goods.

Wall Street '29 — a crash course in things going wrong...

Speculating on the stock market means trying to make money by <u>buying and selling shares</u>. When it all went wrong, <u>everybody suffered</u> because of the awful effect on the economy...

Revision Summary

You've read the section, now try these revision questions, just to check that you've got the whole thing stored safely in your brain. Don't forget — if you get any wrong, look back through the section, learn it properly and then try again...

1) Which American President came up with the Fourteen Points?
2) Name the policy followed by the USA in its dealings with other countries after the First World War.
3) Write a short paragraph explaining why many people in America didn't want to join the League of Nations.
4) Who became President in 1921?
5) What did the Fordney-McCumber Tariff allow the US President to do?
6) How did the Republican government's policies encourage the economic boom in the 1920s?
7) Explain how the motor industry contributed to American prosperity in the 1920s.
8) Why did the increasing numbers of cars and trucks hurt the coal industry?
9) Why did agriculture not share in the boom?
10) Why were there protests about the trial of Sacco and Vanzetti?
11) What did the Ku Klux Klan believe in? Who did they persecute?
12) What were the 'Jim Crow Laws'?
13) When was Prohibition introduced?
14) Explain the following terms: speakeasy, rum-running, moonshine.
15) What crime was Al Capone convicted of in 1931?
16) What problems led to the ending of Prohibition?
17) Name three forms of entertainment which first became popular in the 1920s.
18) Explain how the social position of women changed in the 1920s.
19) What year did the Wall Street Crash happen?
20) Explain four economic problems that contributed to the Wall Street Crash.

The Struggle for Power

Lenin died in 1924 — creating a <u>vacancy</u> at the top of the Communist Party. Stalin organised his funeral, and against Lenin's own wishes, his body was <u>embalmed</u> and placed on <u>public display</u> in Moscow.

Several Leaders Struggled to Succeed Lenin

1) <u>TROTSKY</u> was the most able, and <u>popular</u> with the <u>army</u> and <u>Party members</u>. He led the Red Army brilliantly during the civil war, but some people thought he was too <u>arrogant</u> and he lacked support in the Politburo. He had been a <u>Menshevik</u> and he often made enemies.

2) <u>ZINOVIEV</u> and <u>KAMENEV</u> were left-wingers who agreed with Trotsky's ideas about <u>state control</u> of land and continuing the <u>revolution</u>. But they were determined to <u>stop Trotsky</u> becoming Party leader. Zinoviev was a popular man and had been a friend of Lenin.

3) <u>STALIN</u> didn't seem likely to lead the party. He had accumulated power through <u>good organisation</u> 'behind the scenes' in his work as <u>General Secretary</u> of the Party.

Lenin's testament talked about who might succeed him — he said <u>Trotsky</u> was <u>arrogant</u> but <u>able</u> and said <u>Stalin</u> should be <u>removed from office</u> because he was <u>too rude</u> and <u>ambitious</u>.

Trotsky and Stalin Had a War of Ideas

Leon Trotsky

...wanted <u>revolution</u> to <u>spread</u> to other countries — he called for the USSR to work for a world revolution.

Joseph Stalin

...and most of the Party wanted a period of <u>peace</u> and <u>rebuilding</u> in the USSR — 'Communism in one country'.

How Stalin Made Himself All-Powerful

1) Stalin controlled the Communist Party — he <u>appointed</u> people <u>loyal</u> to him to senior positions.
2) This meant Stalin's <u>rivals</u> had <u>no support</u> in the Party, and he <u>suppressed</u> Lenin's testament.
3) Only <u>Party members</u> could hold <u>government positions</u> and they were <u>chosen</u> by Party <u>voting</u>. It was a <u>one-party state</u>.
4) By the late 1920s Stalin had enough Party support to have his <u>rivals voted out</u> of power.

Stalin Destroyed the Leftists and the Rightists

1) Stalin <u>joined</u> Zinoviev and Kamenev <u>against</u> Trotsky — who was dismissed as Commissar for War in 1925. '<u>Socialism in one country</u>' became Party policy in 1925.
2) Trotsky was isolated — and <u>thrown out</u> of the Communist Party in 1927.
3) <u>New</u> members were elected to the Politburo, <u>loyal</u> to Stalin. At this time Stalin <u>supported the NEP</u> (see p.46) and gradual reform of the economy. The '<u>leftist</u>' Zinoviev and Kamenev were <u>dismissed</u> from the Politburo because they believed in <u>fast economic modernisation</u> (one of Trotsky's main ideas). They joined Trotsky to protest against Stalin and were expelled from the Party.
4) Trotsky was <u>exiled</u> to Kazakhstan in 1928, and forced to <u>leave</u> the USSR in 1929.
5) But in 1928 Stalin adopted <u>fast modernisation</u> instead of the NEP. This swing to the left meant he could now <u>remove</u> the leading figures on the <u>right</u> of the party, such as Bukharin and Rykov who supported the NEP, and could have been a threat to his position.
6) By 1929 he was in <u>complete control</u> as leader of the Communist Party and the USSR.

Stalin was a spin doctor — he changed the revolution...

The key factor in Stalin's rise was <u>Party control</u>. Remember, the Party <u>wasn't</u> the same as the government. But the USSR's constitution could be <u>abused</u> by anyone controlling the Party.

The Terror and the Purges

Stalin was single-minded on his way to the top — and terrifying when he got there.

Stalin was Ruthless in Destroying Rivals

1) Born in 1879 in the Republic of Georgia, his real name was Joseph Jughashvili. He had studied to become a priest, but became a Bolshevik. He changed his name to Stalin ('man of steel') when he was imprisoned as a revolutionary.

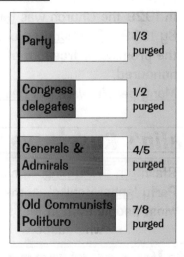

2) He was an organiser who began by making speeches and organising strikes and bank raids to aid Bolshevik funds. He was efficient at routine organisation which many thought was dull.

3) His power base came from being General Secretary of the Party after 1922 — by controlling Party appointments he could control who was given government roles, and chose people loyal to him.

4) By 1930 he was undisputed leader of Russia, but he became terrified that others wanted to overthrow him — this made him determined to get rid of rivals.

The Kirov Murder Began a Purge

1) Kirov was the popular head of the Party in Leningrad — he was murdered in 1934.

2) Some historians think Stalin was responsible for his death — in 1956 Stalin's successor, Khrushchev, blamed Stalin for the murder, but there is no clear proof.

3) Immediately Stalin ordered a purge of people he believed were involved in a conspiracy against Kirov and against himself — but Kirov's murderer was never put on trial.

4) In 1935-6, many 'old' communists like Zinoviev and Kamenev were arrested and charged in 'show trials'. They were forced by torture or threats to confess to betraying Stalin.

5) No one knows exactly what was true and what was invented by Stalin's torturers.

6) One claim was that the exiled Trotsky was plotting with senior leaders to take power.

Soon the Purges Reached Ordinary People

1) Anyone suspected of disloyalty to Stalin was taken away by the NKVD (the new secret police).

2) Most were shot or sent to labour camps.

3) People who wanted to avoid arrest did so by providing information about others — even if it was false.

4) Stalin's wife killed herself (or was murdered) after a purge at the university where she was a teacher.

5) The exiled Trotsky condemned Stalin's purges from his home in Mexico, calling for a new revolution. In 1940 he was murdered by one of Stalin's agents.

6) The total number of people killed by Stalin's regime is uncertain — but some estimates are as high as ten million.

	Purged
Party	1/3 purged
Congress delegates	1/2 purged
Generals & Admirals	4/5 purged
Old Communists Politburo	7/8 purged

The purges — a vicious circle...

Confusing stuff — but you need to get it straight. Under torture people invented all sorts of things to try to save themselves. Stalin started to believe there really was a plot against him.

Section 10 — The USSR 1924-1941

Stalin the Dictator

Stalin <u>tightened</u> his brutal grip on the USSR.

Stalin Controlled all Information

1) Artists and writers had to <u>follow</u> the <u>Party line</u>, creating 'useful' art for the workers.
2) Newspapers, cinema and radio spread <u>propaganda</u> about the <u>heroic workers' struggle</u> and Stalin's great <u>leadership</u> and <u>personality</u>. Criticism was <u>banned</u>.
3) <u>History</u> was <u>rewritten</u> so that Stalin became more <u>important</u> in the story of the October Revolution than he really had been at the time.
4) <u>Trotsky</u> became a '<u>non-person</u>' — his name was removed from history books and articles, and his picture was rubbed out of old photos as though he had never existed.
5) <u>Photographs</u> were <u>altered</u> to show Stalin as a close friend and ally of Lenin.

> <u>Top Tip</u>: Source material in the exams could be <u>propaganda</u> — opinion and not just fact. To get top marks you've got to say which points are true and which aren't, and explain what <u>opinion</u> the source expresses.

The Purges Weakened the USSR

The terror slowed down by the end of the 1930s, but it had <u>serious consequences</u>:

1) Many of the most gifted and able citizens had <u>disappeared</u> — killed or sent to camps.
2) The <u>army</u> and <u>navy</u> was seriously <u>weakened</u> by the loss of most senior officers.
3) Industrial and technical <u>progress</u> was <u>hampered</u> by the loss of top scientists and engineers.
4) In 1936 a <u>new constitution</u> was brought in — every four years there were elections and only official Party candidates were allowed to stand. Power was kept in the Politburo.

The communists Attacked the Church

1) The Russian Orthodox Church had been a powerful <u>supporter</u> of the <u>Tsar</u>.
2) The communist <u>government</u> began to <u>take</u> Church property and land — these were valuable assets for the Party. Christians were persecuted as a political threat to communism and priests were <u>murdered</u> or <u>exiled</u>.
3) In 1929 the Church was <u>banned</u> from any activity except leading worship.
4) By 1939 a <u>few hundred</u> churches <u>remained active</u> — the state claimed the promise of freedom of conscience in the 1936 constitution was being honoured.
5) <u>Many</u> people were <u>still believers</u> — nearly half the population in 1940.

Stalin's Russia was a Dictatorship

1) Stalin <u>ran everything</u> — his policies were often completely different from communist ideas.
2) Party '<u>apparatchiks</u>' — members loyal to Stalin — received <u>privileges</u> like holidays, flats etc.
3) Most people lived in <u>fear</u> but were <u>unable</u> to speak out.

Stalin got stronger — the USSR suffered...

Sources often mix facts with opinions. Your job is to <u>separate</u> the two, and find out why a source gives a particular <u>opinion</u>, and why it may <u>ignore</u> some of the facts. Think about <u>who</u> wrote it, <u>why</u> they wrote it, and <u>when</u> they wrote it — how much they <u>really</u> knew.

Section 10 — The USSR 1924-1941

The Five-Year Plans

The Party used targets to <u>increase the pace</u> of industrialisation.

The USSR still had a Poor Economy

1) The NEP had made some progress, but more rapid <u>growth</u> was <u>needed</u> for the USSR to <u>catch up</u> with the industrialised West and its economies.
2) Stalin adopted Trotsky's ideas for a programme of <u>fast state-controlled modernisation</u> to speed up production. Lenin's policy of the NEP was dropped.
3) The state took over planning for industry and agriculture with a commission called <u>Gosplan</u> to set targets for achievement.

The First Five-Year Plan was started in 1928

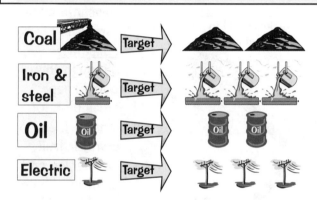

1) A <u>Five-Year Plan</u> set <u>targets</u> for all basic industrial factories and workers.
2) The plan concentrated on basic <u>heavy industry</u> — coal, steel, railways, electricity, machinery.
3) Actual <u>production</u> figures were <u>lower</u> than the targets, but remarkable <u>growth</u> in <u>output</u> was achieved.

In 1933 a Second Five-Year Plan was Started

1) Some parts of the second plan were achieved, but <u>fear</u> at the rise of Adolf Hitler in Nazi Germany meant more <u>development</u> took place in the <u>armaments</u> industry than any other.
2) A <u>third</u> Five-Year Plan started in 1938, but was even more <u>disrupted</u> by war preparation and the German invasion of 1941.

> In under 10 years, the USSR had almost <u>doubled</u> its industrial output — the price was <u>misery</u> and <u>low living standards</u> for Soviet workers.

There were Serious Problems with the Plans

1) <u>New towns</u>, <u>cities</u> and <u>industrial zones</u> were set up — often with <u>poor quality</u> housing.
2) <u>Long hours</u> were worked for <u>low pay</u>, and higher wages were offered to foreign workers with special skills required to work on new schemes.
3) <u>Bonuses</u> were given for workers who could improve upon production targets as an inspiration to others — e.g. Alexei <u>Stakhanov</u>, whose coal mining team dramatically increased its output — but these were often <u>unrealistic targets</u> for most workers.
4) Much of the work was done by forced <u>labour camps</u> of criminals and political prisoners.
5) The targets were <u>propaganda</u> tools — the government said they'd been broken but often it's hard to tell how much was really achieved and how much was just propaganda.

Five years — I've got a cunning plan...

Communist Party propaganda used Stakhanov as an image of a <u>heroic worker</u> in the press and newsreels. A <u>'Stakhanovite' movement</u> began which encouraged workers to match this ideal.

Collectivisation

Communism was <u>forced</u> on the countryside.

Food Production <u>had to be</u> Increased

1) It was vital to <u>increase</u> the <u>food supplies</u> to workers in the towns and cities or the five-year plans <u>wouldn't</u> succeed.
2) Millions of peasants <u>hid</u> food away and <u>didn't support</u> the communists.
3) They were often <u>poor</u> and had no time-saving equipment.
4) Many richer peasants, or <u>kulaks</u> (see p.39), were <u>influential</u> in the villages, which annoyed the local Communist Party secretaries.

In 1929 Stalin began <u>Collectivising All Farms</u>

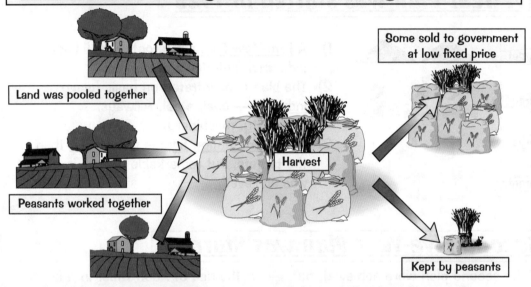

Land was pooled together

Peasants worked together

Harvest

Some sold to government at low fixed price

Kept by peasants

Peasants were forced to <u>collectivise</u> — although they could keep small plots of land of their own for fruit, vegetables and animals. There would now be <u>extra machinery</u> for use on the larger farms.

There were <u>Problems</u> with Collectivisation

1) The <u>speed</u> of change required would <u>destroy</u> the <u>traditional</u> peasant way of life.
2) The peasants <u>resisted</u> this change and didn't want to give up land — especially the kulaks.
3) The collectives were forced to grow <u>particular crops</u> needed for industry, export or food for workers and they had to supply a <u>specific amount</u> to the state, whether the harvest was good or bad. <u>Party officials</u> were brought in to run collectives — this was <u>resented</u>.

Stalin Declared War <u>on the</u> Kulaks

1) Some of the peasants <u>refused</u> to collectivise, and Stalin <u>blamed</u> the <u>kulaks</u>.
2) Stalin sent troops to <u>attack</u> what he called these 'enemies of the people'.
3) An estimated 3 million kulaks were killed. Some were <u>shot</u>. Others died from <u>starvation</u> or cold either on the way to <u>labour camps</u> or during their time working there.
4) Some villages were <u>surrounded</u> and <u>destroyed</u> — many kulaks <u>burned</u> their own crops and <u>killed</u> livestock in protest. This contributed to a <u>famine</u> in the Ukraine — around 5 million people died.
5) 1930 saw famine and a poor harvest, and <u>collectivisation</u> was <u>halted</u> briefly.

Putting the farms together — a collective disaster...

This is all pretty vicious I'm afraid — and it's going to get worse. <u>Collectivisation</u> is a really important topic — it was intended to <u>help</u> the five-year plans but the effects were horrific. Don't forget to learn the <u>main problems</u> with collectivisation. And remember that when things went wrong Stalin looked for someone to blame — the <u>kulaks</u> were scapegoats here.

The Results of Collectivisation

Collectivisation brought agriculture under communist control — but at a cost.

The Famine Continued into 1932-33

Millions were dead or deported. Grain production was down and animal numbers had fallen.

After 1931 collectivisation Began Again

1) By 1939 it was almost complete — 99% of farming land had been collectivised.
2) The kulaks had been eliminated and the peasants left were afraid of communist power.
3) The Communist Party held absolute authority throughout rural Russia as it did in the cities.

There were Pros and Cons to collectivisation

In exam questions you may be presented with different interpretations of this issue.
Remember often these are opinions, mixing facts and ideas, and not always telling the truth:

The Positive View

1) It ended the forced exploitation of peasants by greedy landlords and got rid of the greedy and troublesome kulaks.
2) It helped peasants work together.
3) It provided large-scale organisation of food production for the farms.
4) This was communism in practice.
5) Soviet propaganda showed collective farms as a triumph for the state, and created a myth of the happy worker.

The Negative View

1) The changes were enforced by the army and by law — there was no choice.
2) The kulaks were scapegoats for inefficient food production in the past.
3) The policy led to the murder and imprisonment of millions of people.
4) The new system didn't work at first and a bad harvest combined with kulaks destroying crops and animals caused a serious famine — killing more people.

State Farms were an Extension of Collective Farms

1) Land was owned completely by the state, and peasants worked as labourers — so they received wages even if the farm did badly.
2) Food was delivered to the state, and farm workers bought food with their wages.
3) This was closer to the communist ideal than the collective, but they were very expensive to establish and run. Few farms of this type existed by 1940.

Propaganda and scapegoats — Stalin's key tactics...

Another important page for you to learn here — two views of collectivisation. Remember that neither side is giving pure facts — they're mixing them with opinions. It'll be up to you to tell opinions and facts apart in the exam, and use them to give a balanced answer to the question.

Revision Summary

A section of sweeping changes. Make sure you get to grips with the big bits —
collectivisation, the Five-Year Plans — as well as the nasty political infighting that helped get
Stalin to the top. Once again there are some cheeky little revision questions to help you get to
know it all.

1) What was the main difference in ideas between Stalin and Trotsky?

2) Why was Joseph Stalin able to win the struggle for power?

3) Where was Stalin born?

4) What were the purges?

5) Whose murder sparked off the purges?

6) What was the NKVD?

7) How did Stalin try to change Trotsky's profile in history?

8) How was the Church affected by Stalin's rule?

9) Explain or make a diagram to show the aims of the first Five-Year Plan.

10) What was the name of the commission charged with setting targets for the Five-Year Plans?

11) Why is it hard to tell how much was achieved under the Five-Year Plans?

12) Why were many peasants opposed to a collective farm system?

13) In what year was the drive to collectivise all farms started?

14) Make summary notes/diagrams to explain how a collective farm worked.

15) Why did Stalin want to get rid of the 'kulaks' in the countryside?

16) Which of the Soviet republics suffered from a terrible famine during collectivisation?

17) Give three reasons why some people thought collectivisation was a good thing.

18) Give three reasons why some people thought collectivisation was a bad thing.

19) What was a state farm?

The Rise of the Nazis

The Depression (see p.11) hit Germany hard. The popularity of the Nazi Party soared as a result — people thought the Weimar government couldn't sort out Germany's problems.

The Great Depression caused Poverty and Suffering

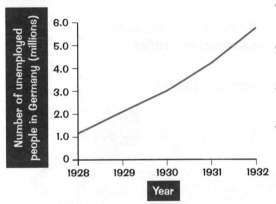

1) The Depression caused massive unemployment in Germany — over 6 million were unemployed by 1933.
2) In 1931, Germany's biggest bank collapsed. This made paying reparations (see p.7) more difficult.
3) Weimar governments kept changing during this time, but none managed to solve the economic problems.
4) The Depression contributed to the collapse of the Weimar Republic. People hoped a new government could sort out the problems.
5) Extremist groups like the Nazis became more popular — they promised strong leadership.

The Nazis increased in Popularity during the Depression

1) The Nazis promised prosperity and to make Germany great again. This appealed to many of the unemployed, as well as to businessmen and young people.
2) Some people supported the Nazis' anti-communist and anti-Jewish views.
3) By 1930, Nazi membership grew to over 300 000.

The Elections of 1930 showed Nazi Gains

Chancellor Heinrich Brüning couldn't control the Reichstag properly — there was a big increase in seats for both the Nazis (who won 107) and the communists (who won 77). Brüning had to rule by emergency decree as no single party had enough seats to control the Reichstag.

Germany had No strong Government

1) By April 1932, conditions were serious in Germany. Millions were unemployed, and the country was desperate for a strong government.
2) President Hindenburg had to stand for re-election, because his term of office had run out. Hitler stood against him, and there was also a communist candidate.
3) Hindenburg, a national hero, said he'd win easily, but didn't win a majority in the first election — in the second ballot he won 53%, beating Hitler's 36.8% of the vote.

Another depressing page...

In normal circumstances, the Nazis would have stayed a small, extremist group on the fringes of politics. Unfortunately the Depression gave them an opportunity to gain mainstream popularity.

The Rise of the Nazis

The Nazis gained a lot of votes — but they used some underhand tactics to get them...

Hindenburg Refused to give the Nazis Power

1) Hindenburg couldn't find a Chancellor who had support in the Reichstag.
2) He appointed the inexperienced Franz von Papen.
3) In the July 1932 Reichstag elections, the Nazis won 230 seats — they were now the biggest party, but didn't have a majority in the Reichstag. Hitler demanded to be made Chancellor.
4) Hindenburg refused because he didn't trust Hitler and kept von Papen.

HITLER'S CLIMB TO POWER

January 1932 — July 1932 — January 1933

- 6 million unemployed
- Hitler uses the Depression to promise better things...
- Stands against Hindenburg in 1932 and loses
- Nazis largest party in Reichstag - July 1932 = 230 seats
- Nazis lose seats in November 1932 but still largest party
- Hitler finally offered 'Chancellorship' in 1933

The Nazis Lost Seats in the Elections

1) The Nazis lost 34 seats in the November 1932 election — they seemed to be losing popularity.
2) Hindenburg appointed Kurt von Schleicher as Chancellor. Von Schleicher tried to cause divisions in the Nazi Party by asking another leading Nazi to be Vice-Chancellor — Gregor Strasser. But Hitler stopped Strasser accepting.
3) Soon, Hindenburg gave in, and offered Hitler the post of Chancellor in January 1933.
4) Hitler decided to call for another election in March 1933, hoping to make the Nazis stronger in the Reichstag.

The Nazis used Dirty Tricks to Win in 1933

The Nazis did well in the elections because:

1) They controlled the news media.
2) Opposition meetings were banned.
3) They used the SA to terrorise opponents.
4) A fire broke out in the Reichstag building, and Hitler whipped up opposition against the communists, who he said started it. Mass arrests of communists followed.
5) Hitler was allowed emergency decrees to deal with the situation — and used these powers to intimidate communist voters.

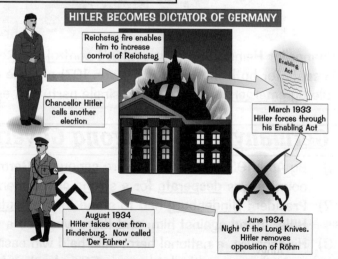

HITLER BECOMES DICTATOR OF GERMANY

Chancellor Hitler calls another election

Reichstag fire enables him to increase control of Reichstag

March 1933 Hitler forces through his Enabling Act

Enabling Act

August 1934 Hitler takes over from Hindenburg. Now called 'Der Führer'.

June 1934 Night of the Long Knives. Hitler removes opposition of Röhm

Germany 1930-33 — a state of confusion...

Loads of facts here — but you don't need to learn them all by heart. The key point is the sequence of events. Hitler didn't come to power overnight — his support increased as the economy got worse and as the other political parties failed to solve Germany's problems.

Hitler Comes to Power

Once Hitler was Chancellor he set about strengthening his power...

Hitler Changed the Law to Keep Control

1) The Nazis won 288 seats but no majority — the communists still won 81.
2) So Hitler declared the Communist Party illegal.
3) This gave him enough support in parliament to bring in an Enabling Bill which was passed with threats and bargaining in March 1933.
4) This bill let him govern for four years without parliament and made all other parties illegal. Hitler was almost in full control.

The Night of the Long Knives

1) Hitler still had opposition — and was worried about rivals within the Nazi party.
2) The biggest threat was Ernst Röhm, who controlled the SA (over 400 000 men). On the 29th-30th June 1934, Hitler sent his own men to arrest Röhm and others. This became known as the 'Night of the Long Knives'.
3) Several hundred people were killed, including Röhm, Strasser and von Schleicher. Any potential opposition had been stamped out.
4) A month later Hindenburg died. Hitler combined the posts of Chancellor and President, made himself Commander-in-Chief of the army, and was called Der Führer (the leader). It was the beginning of dictatorship.

Germany was now under Strong Leaders

1) Germany was reorganised into a number of provinces. Each province was called a Gau (plural: Gaue), with a Gauleiter — a loyal Nazi — in charge of each.
2) Above them were the Reichsleiters who advised Hitler, e.g. Goebbels, who was in charge of propaganda, and Himmler, who was chief of the German police.
3) At the top was the Führer — Hitler himself — who was in absolute control.
4) Every aspect of life was carefully controlled, and only loyal Nazis could be successful.

Joseph Goebbels

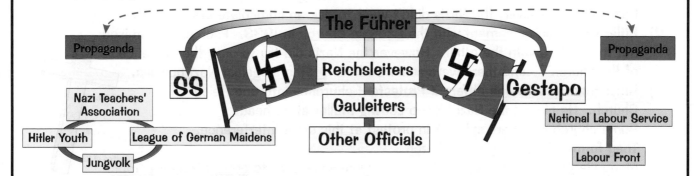

Hitler was obsessed with power...

Once elected, the Nazis pretty quickly turned Germany from a democracy into a dictatorship. Hitler set himself up as a supreme ruler — Chancellor, President and army chief combined.

Nazi Methods of Control

The Nazis used many methods to control the German people — from persuasion to violence...

The Nazis used Propaganda

Propaganda means spreading particular ideas and points of view to try to control how people think. Nazi propaganda blamed the Jews and communists for most of Germany's problems.

1) The Nazis took over the media. They controlled radio broadcasts, and also used films and posters to spread their messages.
2) The Ministry of Public Enlightenment and Propaganda (founded in 1933) was led by Dr Joseph Goebbels. All artists, writers, journalists and musicians had to register to get their work approved.
3) The Nazis organised huge rallies of party members to present an image of power and popularity. They also used the 1936 Berlin Olympics as an opportunity for international publicity.

The Nazis used Censorship

1) The Nazis censored books, newspapers and other material.
2) Those who published anti-Nazi material risked execution.
3) The Nazis used censorship to encourage nationalism and anti-Semitism (hatred of Jews). They praised patriotic German composers such as Wagner but banned the work of Jewish composers such as Mendelssohn.

Germany became a Police State

1) The SS (Schutzstaffel) began as a bodyguard for Hitler. It expanded massively under the leadership of Himmler during the 1930s. Its members were totally loyal to Hitler, and were feared for their cruelty. Himmler was also in charge of the secret police — the Gestapo.
2) After 1933 concentration camps spread across Germany and its territories to hold political prisoners and anybody else considered dangerous to the Nazis. Some of these were later turned into death camps (see p.76).
3) Local wardens were employed to make sure Germans were loyal to the Nazis. People were encouraged to report disloyalty. Many were arrested by the Gestapo as a result.

The Nazis saw the Church as a Threat

1) Many Nazis were against Christianity — its teaching of peace was seen as incompatible with Nazi ideas. However, the Nazis didn't want to risk an immediate attack on it.
2) Hitler signed an agreement with the Catholic Church in 1933. Each side promised not to interfere with the other. However the Nazis did try to curb the influence of the church — and there were some Catholic protests against Nazi policies.
3) Hitler tried to unite the different Protestant churches into one Reich Church. He placed the Nazi Bishop Ludwig Müller at its head. Some church members split off in protest at this state interference. They formed the Confessing Church.
4) Many clergy who stood up to the Nazi regime were sent to concentration camps.

This book wouldn't be available in Nazi Germany...

Imagine if the radio and newspapers all covered the same news in the same way, and featured all the same opinions. You might start to think that way after a while.

Opposition to the Nazis

The Nazis had a tight grip on Germany, but some opposition remained.

Some young people joined the White Rose group

1) The White Rose group was an opposition movement led by students from Munich University between 1942 and 1943. Among the leaders were brother and sister Hans and Sophie Scholl.
2) The group protested against the Nazi discrimination of minorities (see p.76).
3) Some male members of the group had served in the army and had been horrified by the atrocities carried out by the German army, including the mass killing of Jews.
4) They used non-violent methods and distributed anti-Nazi leaflets to encourage opposition.
5) The group were caught and arrested by the Gestapo and several members, including Hans and Sophie Scholl, were tortured and executed.

The Edelweiss Pirates were Difficult to control

1) The Edelweiss Pirates was the name given to groups of rebellious young people which had sprung up across Germany during the 1930s. Groups in different towns each had their own names, including the Navajos and the Roving Dudes.
2) They rejected Nazi values and didn't like being told what to do. They avoided joining the Hitler Youth and some members deliberately got into fights with the Hitler Youth.
3) They were difficult to control because they weren't a single organisation with clear leaders.
4) At first the Nazis mostly ignored them as they had no real political agenda.
5) However, during the 1940s, they started distributing anti-Nazi leaflets. They also helped army deserters, forced labourers and escaped concentration camp prisoners.
6) The Nazis eventually cracked down on the groups. Many were arrested. In 1944, several members of the Edelweiss Pirates in Cologne were publicly hanged.

Members of the Kreisau Circle were Against Violence

1) The Kreisau Circle was an anti-Nazi movement led by Helmuth von Moltke and Yorck von Wartenburg. It was made up of churchmen, scholars and politicians.
2) The group was against violence, so they didn't actively resist the Nazis. Instead they discussed how to make Germany a better country after the Nazis had fallen.
3) Some members of the Circle tried to inform Allied governments about the dangers and weaknesses of Nazi control.
4) In 1944, members of the Kreisau Circle, including Moltke, were arrested and executed.

The Stauffenberg Bomb Plot was an attempt to Kill Hitler

1) By 1944, some German military officers were unhappy with Hitler's leadership — they believed he was going to lead Germany to defeat.
2) Claus von Stauffenberg, along with other German officers, planned to kill Hitler. They wanted to install a moderate government, including members of the Kreisau Circle.
3) On 20 July 1944, Stauffenberg put a bomb in a briefcase and left it in a meeting room by Hitler's chair. However, someone moved the briefcase. Although the bomb exploded, Hitler was unhurt.
4) Most of the plotters, including Stauffenberg, were quickly captured and executed.

Anyone would think Hitler wasn't very popular...

There were plenty of people who weren't keen on Hitler and his policies. Some of them protested peacefully, but others were more violent. Learn all these major movements against Hitler.

German Growth Under the Nazis

The Nazis took strict <u>control</u> of the economy.

Hitler gave Work to 6 Million Unemployed

1) Hitler started a huge <u>programme</u> of <u>public works</u>, which gave <u>jobs</u> to thousands of people.
2) From 1933, huge motorways — <u>autobahns</u> — were started. <u>Unemployment fell</u> dramatically.
3) But — the Nazis also <u>fiddled with the statistics</u> to make unemployment look <u>lower</u> than it really was. E.g. they didn't count women or Jewish people in the unemployment statistics — this is called "<u>invisible unemployment</u>".

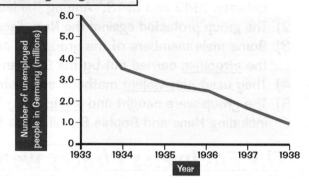

People were Encouraged to Work by Rewards

1) <u>All</u> men between 18 and 25 could be <u>recruited</u> into the <u>National Labour Service</u> and given jobs.
2) The Nazis got rid of trade unions. Instead workers had to join the Nazis' <u>Labour Front</u>.
3) The Nazis introduced '<u>Strength through Joy</u>' — a scheme which provided workers with <u>cheap holidays</u> and leisure activities. Another scheme, '<u>Beauty of Labour</u>', encouraged factory owners to <u>improve conditions</u> for their workers.
4) Output increased in Germany, and <u>unemployment</u> was almost <u>ended</u> completely. The Nazis introduced the <u>Volkswagen</u> (the people's car) as an <u>ambition</u> for people to aim for.

5) <u>Wages</u> were still relatively <u>low</u> though — and workers <u>weren't allowed</u> to go on <u>strike</u> or campaign for better conditions.

Hitler Re-armed the German Military

1) Another way to create work was to <u>build up</u> the armed forces. The Nazis did this <u>secretly</u> at first, because the <u>Treaty of Versailles</u> had <u>banned</u> it.
2) Hitler <u>sacked</u> some of the generals, and <u>replaced</u> them with Nazi supporters. Goering was put in charge of the newly-formed <u>Luftwaffe</u> (airforce), which had been banned at Versailles.
3) In 1935, <u>military conscription</u> was reintroduced (drafting men into the army).
4) In 1936, the Nazis introduced a <u>Four-Year Plan</u> to <u>prepare</u> the country for <u>war</u>. <u>Industrial production</u> increased — many workers had to <u>retrain</u> in jobs that would help the war effort. The plan was to make Germany <u>self-sufficient</u>, so it wasn't reliant on foreign goods.

Hitler reduced unemployment — and gained popularity...

Hitler provided new jobs and helped Germany recover from the <u>Depression</u> (see p.69).
The <u>economic recovery</u> was one of the main reasons the Nazis managed to stay in power.

Young People and Women

The Nazis believed that to control the future they had to <u>influence</u> children and their mothers.

The Nazis created powerful Youth Groups

1) Hitler knew that <u>loyalty</u> from <u>young people</u> was essential if the Nazis were to remain <u>strong</u>.
2) Boys aged fourteen upwards were recruited to the <u>Hitler Youth</u>, which was <u>compulsory</u> from <u>1939</u>. Girls aged from fourteen joined the <u>League of German Maidens</u>.
3) Boys wore <u>military-style uniforms</u>, and took part in lots of <u>physical exercise</u>. Girls were mainly trained in <u>domestic skills</u> like <u>sewing</u>.
4) The boys were being prepared to be <u>soldiers</u>, the girls to be <u>wives</u> and <u>mothers</u>.

The Nazis took over Education

1) Schools started teaching <u>Nazi propaganda</u>. Jews were banned from <u>teaching</u> in <u>schools</u> and <u>universities</u>. Most teachers joined the <u>Nazi Teachers' Association</u> and were trained in Nazi methods. Children had to <u>report</u> teachers who did not use them.
2) Subjects like history and biology were <u>rewritten</u> to fit in with Nazi ideas. Children were taught to be <u>anti-Semitic</u> and that <u>World War I</u> was lost because of Jews and communists.
3) <u>Physical education</u> became more important for boys, who sometimes played <u>war games</u> with live ammunition.
4) In universities students <u>burned</u> anti-Nazi and Jewish books, and <u>Jewish lecturers</u> were sacked.

Women were expected to raise Large Families

1) Nazis didn't want <u>women</u> to have too much freedom. They believed the role of women was to support their families at home. Women existed to provide children.
2) The <u>League of German Maidens</u> spread the Nazi idea that it was an honour to produce <u>large families</u> for Germany. Nazis gave <u>awards</u> to women for doing this.
3) At school, girls studied subjects like <u>cookery</u>. It was stressed that they should choose <u>'Aryan' husbands</u>.
4) Women were <u>banned</u> from being <u>lawyers</u> in 1936 and the Nazis did their best to stop them following other professions. The <u>shortage of workers</u> after 1937 meant more women had to <u>go back to work</u>. Many Nazi men did not like this.

Eight main Reasons for Hitler's Popularity

It's hard to imagine now, but the Nazis were <u>genuinely popular</u> with many Germans at the time.

1) He gave the Germans <u>jobs</u> after the struggles and unemployment of the 1920s.
2) The people were <u>taught</u> the Nazi way from an <u>early</u> age.
3) He made them <u>proud</u> internationally — Germans had felt humiliated for a long time.
4) People felt much <u>better off</u> as industry expanded.
5) Massive <u>rallies</u> every year gave the <u>impression</u> of a strong, prosperous nation.
6) The <u>army supported</u> Hitler's aim to make Germany strong again.
7) Businesses liked the <u>prosperity</u> and the way Hitler attacked the communists.
8) People were <u>frightened</u> to protest against Nazi methods — they knew they'd be arrested.

Hitler Youth — not like your local youth club, then...

Although the Nazis were <u>destroyed</u> in 1945, they expected to be in power a lot, lot longer. That's why they spent so much time and effort on the <u>young</u> — creating Nazis for the <u>future</u>.

Persecution

The <u>Holocaust</u> was the persecution and <u>mass murder</u> of Jewish people by the Nazis.

Hitler believed Aryans were a Super-Race

1) The Nazis believed <u>Aryans</u> (whites) were the '<u>master race</u>' and people of other ethnicities, like Jewish or Slavic people, were <u>inferior</u>.
2) The Nazis <u>blamed</u> Jewish people for <u>problems</u> in <u>German society</u>.
3) The Nazis wanted a German population of only '<u>pure</u>' Aryan people who fitted their ideal. They wanted to <u>eliminate</u> people who were disabled, homosexual, held different beliefs, or weren't 'Aryan'.
4) Hitler was <u>angry</u> when an <u>African-American</u> called <u>Jesse Owens</u> took <u>four gold medals</u> at the <u>1936 Berlin Olympics</u>, and when the German World Heavyweight Boxing Champion Max Schmeling was beaten by another African American, <u>Joe Louis</u>.

Persecution of the Jews Increased through the 1930s

In 1935 Hitler passed the Nuremberg Laws

1) These laws <u>stopped</u> Jews being <u>German citizens</u>.
2) They <u>banned marriage</u> between Jews and non-Jews in Germany.
3) They <u>banned sexual relationships</u> between Jews and non-Jews.

Kristallnacht 1938 — the Night of Broken Glass

1) A <u>Jew murdered</u> a German <u>diplomat</u> in Paris in November 1938.
2) There was <u>rioting</u> throughout Germany — thousands of Jewish shops were <u>smashed</u>, and thousands of Jews were <u>arrested</u>.

Jewish people were Moved to Ghettos

1) After the invasions of Poland and Russia <u>more</u> Jews came under Nazi control.
2) From 1940, Jewish people were forced to move into <u>ghettos</u> — separate districts of cities which were usually <u>walled in</u> and policed by <u>armed guards</u>. The largest was in <u>Warsaw</u>.
3) Conditions in the ghettos were terrible. <u>Starvation</u> and <u>disease</u> killed thousands. A rebellion in the Warsaw ghetto in 1943 was ruthlessly put down.
4) When Russia was invaded in 1941, soldiers followed with orders to <u>kill</u> every Jew they came across in the occupied towns and villages.

The Nazis began the Final Solution in 1942

1) The <u>Final Solution</u> was the Nazis' plan to <u>destroy</u> the Jewish people.
2) <u>Death camps</u> were built in Eastern Europe. <u>Gas chambers</u> were built for mass murder.
3) Mainly Jewish people were killed, but <u>other</u> groups were targeted as well, for example Slavs (Russians and Poles), Roma, black people, homosexuals, disabled people and communists.
4) <u>Heinrich Himmler</u>, head of the SS, was in overall charge of this 'Final Solution'.
5) Some death camps were: <u>Auschwitz</u>, <u>Treblinka</u>, <u>Sobibor</u>, <u>Chelmno</u>, <u>Belzec</u>.
6) By the end of the war, approximately <u>6 million Jewish people</u> had been killed by the Nazis.

Nazi Germany — a climate of cruelty and fear...

The Jewish people <u>suffered terribly</u> at the hands of the Nazis — and you need to know how. This is horrific, and it's hard for us to understand how such cruelty could have been carried out. Remember — other groups were also persecuted including Roma (gypsies) and the disabled.

Impacts of the Second World War

The Second World War had a big impact on German society.

The War forced Changes in the German Economy

1) In 1936, Goering introduced a Four-Year Plan to prepare the German economy for war.
2) The Nazis built up industries like weapons and chemicals at the expense of domestic goods.
3) By the outbreak of war, a quarter of the work force was working in war industries, especially weapons. Two years later, this had become three-quarters. Unemployment fell.
4) During the war, working hours increased to over 50 hours a week, and wages were lower than they had been under the Weimar Republic. Despite this, the German industry was not producing enough, and there were not enough workers.
5) Industry suffered as a result of the bombings. Industrial plants were bombed, particularly in the Ruhr, meaning factories had to be rebuilt.
6) In 1943, Albert Speer was appointed Minister for Armaments and Production. He reorganised industry and rapidly increased production, but the German industry still couldn't produce enough.
7) A lot of working age Germans were conscripted into the army, so the Nazis used foreign workers to help keep the economy going. By 1944, around 20% of the workforce were foreigners — either civilians from occupied territories or prisoners of war.
8) At the start of the war, the Nazis had encouraged women not to work. However, by 1944 about 50% of the workforce were women.

The War Affected German Civilians

Bombings killed many civilians

1) From 1942, the Allies began to bomb German cities more heavily. Around half a million German civilians were killed, and many more were made homeless.
2) The bombing was often relentless — the US bombed by day and Britain bombed by night.
3) The German cities of Dresden, Berlin and Hamburg were all badly affected by bombing.

Rationing affected quality of life

1) Food and clothes rationing began in 1939, but while Germany was winning the war, most goods could still be acquired easily.
2) By 1942, German civilians were living off much less than British civilians. Civilians lived off rations of bread, vegetables and potatoes — these rations decreased as the war progressed.
3) It became nearly impossible to buy new clothes or shoes.

Propaganda encouraged loyalty to the Nazis

1) Nazi news media only reported wartime successes. This made the Nazis appear strong, but the public were misinformed.
2) Nazi propaganda warned Germans against non-Nazi groups, such as the Bolsheviks. Some people supported the Nazis because they were made to fear the alternatives.
3) In the last days of the war, Nazi propaganda encouraged members of the Nazi party, boys and old men to defend Berlin from the Russians to the last man.

The Second World War was tough on everyone...

There were very few people who were left unaffected by the War. War dominated daily life.

Revision Summary

It's quite a tricky section this. Among other things, you have to get to grips with how the Nazis, who were a small fringe group in the mid 1920s, became the biggest party in the Reichstag by July 1932. The Nazis were in power for twelve years, during which time they massively changed German society and the economy, as well as doing some truly terrible things. These revision questions should help you to remember it all:

1) What happened to Germany's biggest bank in 1931?
2) Who beat Hitler in the presidential elections of April 1932?
3) How did Hitler use the Reichstag Fire?
4) What did Hitler's Enabling Bill allow him to do in March 1933?
5) What was the Night of the Long Knives?
6) What title did Hitler give himself on the death of Hindenburg in 1934?
7) What were Gaue?
8) Which Nazi was put in charge of propaganda? Write about some of the methods he used.
9) What was the SS? What was the Gestapo?
10) Name two groups who opposed the Nazis.
11) Describe the Stauffenberg bomb plot.
12) Give an achievement of the Nazi programme of public works.
13) What was the 'Strength through Joy' programme? What organisation did workers have to join instead of trade unions?
14) Name the leading Nazi who was put in charge of the Luftwaffe.
15) In what ways did the Nazis make sure that young people followed their cause?
16) Which organisation did teachers in Nazi Germany have to join?
17) Give eight reasons why the German people followed the Nazis.
18) Name the African American athlete who won four gold medals at the Berlin Olympics in 1936.
19) What were the Nuremberg Laws? What did they do?
20) Describe what happened on the 'Night of Broken Glass'.
21) Where was the largest Jewish ghetto in Nazi-controlled Europe?
22) What did the Four-Year Plan aim to do?
23) What were the average rations for a German civilian towards the end of the war?

Consequences of the Wall Street Crash

The Wall Street Crash in 1929 (see p.60) destroyed confidence. People lost money and savings and there was no recovery in sight. A second long decline from mid 1931 to early 1933 resulted in even more bankruptcies.

The Depression hit all walks of life

1) Around 20 000 US businesses folded in 1932 alone.
2) By mid-1932 around 5000 banks folded — losing over $3 billion of deposits.
3) The national income fell from over $80bn to as low as $40bn (1929-33).
4) The price of goods continued to fall. Industrial production was cut. Wages fell and workers were laid off. A quarter of the workforce (about 13 million) were unemployed by 1933.
5) Farm product prices fell 60%. It was costing farmers more to harvest and transport their produce than they could make by selling it — fruit rotted, sheep were killed and burnt, wheat was not harvested and debts increased. Many bankrupt farmers were evicted or became tenants, losing their independence.

The Depression caused Terrible Poverty

1) Poverty led to undernourishment.
2) Thousands were made homeless. Some of the homeless built shanty towns to live in. These were nicknamed Hoovervilles after President Hoover.
3) Many people moved to seek work. Some fathers abandoned their families in the search for work.
4) Migrant farm workers roamed the countryside looking for work. Their situation was made worse by a period of drought in the Midwest, partly caused by overuse of the land.
5) Marriages were delayed and the birth rate fell.

TYPICAL DIET DURING THE DEPRESSION

Breakfast
Bread and coffee

Dinner
Bread, carrots and soup

Attempts were made to Help People

The Depression was a shattering and demoralising experience. Some people fought hard for survival and to keep their pride. State and charitable agencies tried to help people keep going.

Private charities, religious groups ⟶
State governments ⟶
Federal relief agencies ⟶

RELIEF AND HELP

⟶ Temporary homes and shelters
⟶ Supply of food and clothes, bread lines and soup kitchens
⟶ Offers of jobs

John Steinbeck's great novel The Grapes of Wrath tells the story of farmers forced to try their luck in California during the Depression. If you haven't got time to read it, try to find a copy of the film to watch — you can feel like you're revising while watching a great movie. (Don't forget to learn this stuff too though).

From bad to worse — more than a little depressing...

The main point on this page is simply that the Depression was really bad, and made lots of people destitute and miserable. That's not enough though — you need to learn the details too.

Election of Roosevelt (FDR)

The Republican President Hoover tried to deal with the Depression — but he <u>failed</u>.

Hoover's Action on the Economy didn't go far enough

Hoover tried some measures to help the economy:

1) Some <u>reduction in taxation</u> so that people had more money to spend.
2) An expansion of '<u>public works</u>'.
3) A <u>Home Loans Act</u> to help with mortgage payments.
4) <u>Conferences</u> with <u>industrialists</u> in an effort to maintain jobs and wages.
5) A one-year <u>suspension on war debts</u> and reparations by European governments to the USA in the hope that this would enable them to buy more American goods.
6) The <u>Reconstruction Finance Corporation</u> provided some loans to help firms.

For many people this was "<u>too little, too late</u>". Hoover persisted in his belief in '<u>rugged individualism</u>' — he believed that if the right conditions could be created, people would be able to <u>work themselves out of poverty</u> without direct assistance from the government. He therefore <u>refused</u> to offer any financial <u>relief</u> to individuals. This was very <u>unpopular</u>.

Some of Hoover's policies may even have harmed the world economy and hampered US recovery. For example, <u>high tariffs on foreign goods</u> led to retaliation — other countries raised their tariffs to <u>protect</u> their <u>own industries</u>. US exports to Europe more than halved between 1929 and 1932.

FDR was Elected in 1932

1) FDR (Franklin Delano Roosevelt) had been a popular <u>governor of New York</u>. He ran a well organised and <u>energetic election campaign</u> supported by wealthy backers. Influential supporters helped him with ideas and well written speeches. So FDR looked like a winner.

2) Hoover wasn't helped by the '<u>Bonus Army</u>' protests in June 1932. 15 000 First World War army veterans gathered in Washington to demand extra bonus payments not due until 1945. Two protesters were killed by police, and many more were injured in army action to clear their encampments.

3) The <u>Democrats</u> swept to <u>power</u>, with FDR gaining 22 million votes and Hoover 15 million.

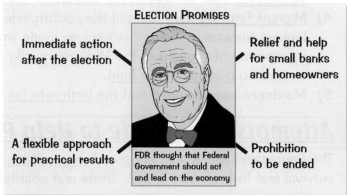

ELECTION PROMISES

Immediate action after the election

Relief and help for small banks and homeowners

A flexible approach for practical results

FDR thought that Federal Government should act and lead on the economy

Prohibition to be ended

FDR had 3 Main Aims

This was to be a '<u>New Deal</u>' for the American people.

<u>Relief</u> — to help to improve the lives of people.
<u>Recovery</u> — to begin to rebuild US industry and trade.
<u>Reform</u> — to change conditions to ensure future progress.

Happy times are here again...

The Great Depression was a terrible time. Hoover tried to help <u>big business</u> and the <u>economy as a whole</u>, but he did little to help <u>ordinary people</u>. That's why he lost to FDR in 1932.

The New Deal

Roosevelt now had to <u>deliver</u> his 'New Deal' to the American people.

Confidence had to be restored in Banking and Finance

1) There was a four-day '<u>bank holiday</u>' closure.
2) Healthy, sound banks <u>reopened</u>. <u>Weak banks</u> were reorganised under Federal supervision.
3) Laws were introduced to <u>insure deposits</u> and <u>limit speculation</u>.
4) The <u>stock market</u> was to be monitored more closely.
5) The USA was taken off the '<u>gold standard</u>'.
6) Bank failures fell — deposits rose — and <u>confidence</u> began to return.

The 'Hundred Days' launched many new measures

The '<u>Hundred Days</u>' was the first period of Roosevelt's term in office, during which he introduced many new acts. Much work was carried out by special <u>Federal agencies</u> (often called '<u>alphabet agencies</u>' because they were known by their initials). The most important were:

FERA The <u>Federal Emergency Relief Administration</u> made $500m available to state and local government for emergency relief. This was used to give direct assistance to the poor, for example: dole payments and soup kitchens.

CCC The <u>Civilian Conservation Corps</u> provided work for thousands of unemployed men in forestry, water and soil conservation projects. This was followed by the <u>Public Works Administration (PWA)</u> which provided work building roads, bridges, hospitals, schools and housing.

AAA The <u>Agricultural Adjustment Administration</u> paid farmers to limit food production. This raised prices and increased incomes. The AAA also helped farmers modernise and rebuild their businesses.

NRA The <u>National Recovery Act</u> drew up codes of fair competition, set minimum wages and a maximum eight-hour day. Trade unions were encouraged. This was a cooperative effort and relied on the voluntary agreement of businesses.

TVA The <u>Tennessee Valley Authority</u> (see p.82 for details).

HOLC The <u>Home Owners' Loan Corporation</u> helped people who were in danger of having their homes repossessed. It provided new long-term loans.

The Economy Strengthened a bit but Problems remained

1) Some agencies gave out money too <u>slowly</u>.
2) Stricter regulations on hours, wages and child labour <u>hurt small businesses and farmers</u>.
3) <u>Tenant farmers</u> continued to suffer — 3 million were displaced from the land (1932-5).
4) There was some <u>opposition to Federal control</u> — for example by the 'Liberty League' (1934-6). The Supreme Court raised <u>constitutional objections</u>, which delayed several of FDR's measures.
5) After an initial increase in industrial production the NRA encountered much opposition from businesses and was <u>unable to secure continued recovery</u>. Some argue that FDR didn't put enough money into reviving industry.
6) The <u>severe drought</u> and heat, on top of overfarming, led to the erosion of topsoil in large areas of the Midwest. Parts of Kansas and Oklahoma became '<u>dust bowls</u>'.

> But the fall in wages and prices was halted. <u>Employment</u> rose and, despite criticisms that Roosevelt was not being radical enough, the measures were very <u>popular</u>.

Learn this and you can have an ice cream — a new deal...

Roosevelt gave speeches on the radio known as '<u>fireside chats</u>'. These urged listeners to have faith in the New Deal. Overall, he gave the American public a big old charm offensive.

The TVA and the Second New Deal

There were still problems left that needed action...

The Tennessee Valley Authority (TVA)

1) The Tennessee Valley was one of the poorest regions in the country. Overcultivation had led to soil erosion and this had turned the land into a near desert.
2) Agriculture was in a dreadful condition and industry almost non-existent. Many local people were leaving the area to find work further west.

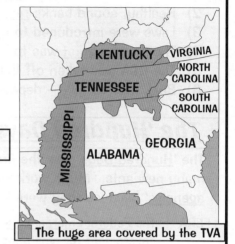

The huge area covered by the TVA

The TVA brought Construction Projects

1) The TVA built a large number of dams to prevent the flooding that had been causing so much damage and to provide irrigation in times of drought.
2) Trees were planted to prevent more soil erosion.
3) The TVA constructed power stations which brought electricity to the area.

There was a huge improvement in the region's economy. The massive building projects provided thousands of jobs for local people. Agriculture began to prosper.

The Second New Deal focused on Social Welfare

The Second New Deal began in 1935 and took the new ideas about social welfare and the responsibilities of the state even further. Roosevelt introduced new measures that would benefit the elderly, the sick and the unemployed.

The Social Security Act was passed in 1935

1) This began America's state system of old age pensions. Americans over 65 received a government pension.
2) It also set up a plan for unemployment benefit. Both employers and employees paid into a fund so that the worker received a small amount of unemployment benefit if they lost their job.
3) It also set up schemes to help the sick and the disabled.

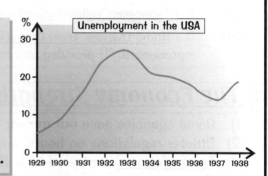

Unemployment in the USA

The Wagner Act, 1935

This act gave workers the right to join a trade union. Companies were now forced by law to allow their employees to become members of a trade union.

The Works Progress Administration (WPA), 1935

This was very like the Public Works Administration, but it also created jobs for actors, artists, photographers and musicians. However, the USA still lagged behind countries like Britain and Germany in social welfare provision.

A new New Deal for y'all to remember...

A big change brought about by the New Deal was the acceptance that the state had a role in relieving the hardship of individual citizens. This was what the second New Deal was all about.

Opposition to the New Deal

Although many Americans supported the New Deal, some people opposed Roosevelt's policies.

Some thought the New Deal had Not Gone Far Enough

1) The politician Senator Huey Long of Louisiana had a plan that he called 'Share Our Wealth'.
2) Long wanted to tax the rich and give the money to the poor. He claimed that it would give every family an income of $5000 a year. The families would spend the money and this would create a bigger demand for goods and services and therefore more jobs.
3) Huey Long planned to stand against FDR in the 1936 presidential elections — but he was assassinated in 1935.

   1) Another of Roosevelt's critics was Dr Francis Townsend. Dr Townsend recommended a plan by which every American over 60 was given a pension of $200 per month (a huge amount in the 1930s) on condition that they spent the lot within one month.
   2) Dr Townsend said that this would give a big boost to the economy and get unemployment down.

Some thought the New Deal had Gone Too Far

Some businessmen and the Republican party took the view that the New Deal had gone too far.

1) Roosevelt's critics said that the New Deal made Americans too dependent on government help. These people believed that it was wrong for the government to create work and give Americans pensions and sickness benefits. Individuals should provide these things for themselves through their own efforts.
2) Some business people were angry that the New Deal allowed trade unions into the workplace. They said this was unnecessary government interference in the way that they ran their business affairs.
3) Some people condemned the New Deal measures as 'socialist' and therefore un-American.
4) It was claimed that it was wrong to tax the rich to pay for the New Deal. The rich had earned their wealth through their own efforts and enterprise. By taxing the rich you discouraged them from wishing to create more wealth. This was a strongly capitalist viewpoint.

There was also Opposition from the Supreme Court

1) In 1935, the Supreme Court declared that several of the New Deal measures were unconstitutional and therefore illegal. Most of the judges were Republicans and therefore opposed to Roosevelt and his policies.
2) Roosevelt asked Congress to allow him to put six Democrats on the Supreme Court so that this would not happen again. However, many Americans felt that this would be a violation of the constitution and Roosevelt was forced to back down.
3) The Supreme Court began to take a more lenient view of the New Deal and the argument died down. However the objections did succeed in delaying some of FDR's policies.

Money, money, money...
America was (and to a great extent still is) attached to ideas of free enterprise and minimal state intervention in the affairs of individuals. This largely explains the opposition to FDR.

How Successful was the New Deal?

In order to assess how <u>successful</u> the New Deal was, you must first remind yourself of what it was <u>trying to accomplish</u> — its three main aims...

The New Deal had considerable success in its Main Aims

Give aid to the needy

1) The <u>FERA</u> did a <u>good job</u> of providing the needy with much-needed <u>emergency aid</u>.
2) From 1935 onwards, the elements of a basic <u>welfare state</u> were established — <u>unemployment benefit</u> and <u>pensions</u> were introduced, and the government intervened to ensure better working conditions and a <u>minimum wage</u>.

Restore stability to America's banking and financial system

1) Roosevelt successfully resolved the <u>banking crisis</u> with the <u>Emergency Banking Act (EBA)</u>.
2) This <u>restored</u> people's <u>confidence</u> in the <u>banks</u> and people began to deposit their money in them once again.

Reduce unemployment and restore prosperity

1) The New Deal created <u>millions of jobs</u> through the various agencies such as the CCC and the PWA. When Roosevelt became President in 1933, unemployment stood at <u>13 million</u>. In 1940, the figure was <u>8 million</u>.
2) However, though the 1940 figure is an improvement on the one for 1933, it is important to remember that there were <u>only 1.5 million people out of work in 1929</u>. So the New Deal did not actually bring back the low unemployment levels of 1920s America.
3) In 1937, another depression hit the American economy and unemployment rose in 1938 to over 10 million. The New Deal therefore <u>failed</u> to solve America's <u>unemployment problem</u>.

World War Two solved the Unemployment Problem

It was the outbreak of the <u>Second World War</u> in Europe that brought the jobless total down.

1) In March 1941 the <u>Lend-Lease Act</u> authorised the President to lease or sell military equipment and supplies to the British and other countries on the Allied side for their fight against Germany. From then on, the US geared production to <u>war needs</u>, eventually supplying her allies with <u>$50 billion</u> worth of food, armaments and equipment.

2) America's entry into the <u>war</u> in December 1941 <u>increased the demand</u> for military equipment. This, together with <u>recruitment</u> into the armed forces, put an end to high unemployment.

The end of the Depression — I feel better already...

Roosevelt achieved quite a lot with the New Deal, but he could not end the Depression, only <u>relieve</u> the worst of the <u>hardship</u>. It took major changes in economic conditions, brought about by the <u>Second World War</u>, to finally sort out America's unemployment problem.

Revision Summary

The Depression was a very difficult time for the US — but it led to some really radical thinking and big efforts to turn things around. These efforts weren't always successful, and they weren't always popular. But they do give you plenty of things to learn about. Speaking of which — here are some revision questions to help you make sure you've learnt it all. Keep repeating them till you can get them all right without having to check back through the section.

1) How many Americans were unemployed by 1933?
2) Why did some farmers not bother to harvest their produce in the early 1930s?
3) What were Hoovervilles?
4) Explain why Hoover lost the 1932 election.
5) Why might Hoover's protectionist policies have damaged the recovery?
6) Which party did Hoover belong to?
7) What were Roosevelt's three main aims after winning the 1932 election?
8) Name three steps that were taken to try to increase confidence in the banking system?
9) What were the 'Hundred Days'?
10) Name three 'alphabet agencies' and explain how they helped America through the Depression.
11) What was the name given to areas of land which lost their topsoil due to drought and overfarming?
12) What does TVA stand for?
13) Write a short summary of the work of the TVA.
14) Name two acts passed in 1935 as part of the 'Second New Deal'.
15) Why did Huey Long oppose the New Deal?
16) Write a short outline of Dr Francis Townsend's plan to combat the Depression.
17) Explain why some businessmen and members of the Republican party opposed the New Deal.
18) Why did the political balance of the Supreme Court hamper the New Deal?
19) To what figure had unemployment fallen in 1940?
20) How successful was the New Deal in achieving its three main aims?
21) What finally solved America's unemployment problem?

Civil Rights after the War

In the 1940s and 1950s, African Americans were still denied the rights promised by the American Constitution. Many states were still segregated (see p.57) and racist attitudes were common.

African Americans fought in World War 2

1) World War 2 started in 1939, but the USA didn't join the fighting until December 1941.
2) About a million African Americans fought in the American armed forces during the war.
3) The army was segregated — African Americans served in separate military units to whites.
4) African Americans saw action on all fronts and often distinguished themselves in the fighting, for example in the Battle of the Bulge in 1944 and at Iwo Jima in 1945.
5) However, because of racism, no African Americans were awarded the Medal of Honor.
6) Some concessions were made for the sake of military efficiency. African Americans were admitted to the Marine Corps for the first time. The first African-American fighter pilots flew combat missions.
7) African-American soldiers fought for freedom abroad — but returned home to a society in which they were oppressed and discriminated against.
8) After the war, in 1948, President Truman ended segregation in the armed forces.

African Americans remained Second-Class Citizens

In 1941, President Roosevelt had signed an executive order banning racial discrimination in defence industries. This caused resentment from some white workers. Race riots broke out in the industrial city of Detroit in 1943 — during which 25 African Americans and 9 white Americans were killed.

In the South of the USA, segregation was enforced by law in most aspects of daily life — schools, restaurants, theatres, workplaces, public transport and public toilets. Most white people thought this was normal and unremarkable. In the North, there was some informal segregation — reflecting and reinforcing African Americans' lower social status. Average wealth and living standards remained comparatively low for African Americans across the whole country.

The Ku Klux Klan (see p.57) was a secret organisation that believed in white supremacy — and used violence to intimidate African Americans. It had declined in popularity by the 1940s but was still active — and many people still shared its beliefs.

Civil Rights — in the land of the not yet free...

Despite gaining freedom from slavery after the civil war, African Americans were still heavily oppressed in the South. See p.57 for more on how prejudice was rife in pre-war America. Make sure you learn about the impact of World War 2, and how bad things remained at home.

Non-Violent Protest and Education

With the help of the <u>Supreme Court</u>, the African Americans began to gain civil rights. But it was a slow process...

Justice lay in Enforcing the Constitution

The USA's <u>Declaration of Independence</u> and <u>Constitution</u> promise <u>all citizens</u> certain <u>rights</u>, including equal protection by the law. One strategy for gaining civil rights for African Americans was to appeal back to these <u>iconic American documents</u>.

Many groups focussed on Non-Violent Protest

A number of non-violent protest groups fought for civil rights:

- The <u>NAACP</u> — National Association for the Advancement of Colored People, founded in 1909 — funded court cases challenging discrimination.
- <u>CORE</u> — the Congress of Racial Equality, founded in 1942 — dedicated to non-violent protest.
- The <u>SCLC</u> — Southern Christian Leadership Conference, founded in 1957 by Martin Luther King and Ralph Abernathy — used the churches' strength for protests.
- The <u>SNCC</u> — Student Nonviolent Coordinating Committee, formed in 1960.

The Supreme Court ruled against Segregated Education

1) Following campaigns by the NAACP, the <u>US Supreme Court</u> — which interprets the Constitution — ruled in the case <u>Brown v Board of Education of Topeka (1954)</u> that <u>racial segregation</u> in <u>state schools</u> was <u>unconstitutional</u>.
2) Since the <u>Constitution</u> is the <u>highest law</u> of the land, the Federal (central) government was obliged to intervene when it was contradicted by <u>local state law</u>.
3) In 1957 President Eisenhower ordered 1000 paratroopers to the <u>Central High School</u> campus at <u>Little Rock</u>, Arkansas, to enforce the admission of <u>nine African-American pupils</u> in the face of local <u>mob violence</u>.
4) In 1962, <u>James Meredith</u>, an African American, had to have the protection of Federal troops as he registered as a student at the <u>University of Mississippi</u>.
5) In both the above cases the <u>state governor</u>, backed by passionate <u>public support</u> from white people for segregation, did all he could to <u>defy</u> the Federal authorities.

All men are created equal...

...or so says the <u>Declaration of Independence</u> which, along with the <u>Constitution</u>, has a lot to say about <u>freedom</u> and <u>equality</u> — but African Americans still had to struggle to achieve theirs. Equal access to <u>education</u> was a key part of the struggle — attempts to <u>desegregate schools</u> would go on into the 1970s, and would be a big source of <u>tension</u>.

The Bus Boycott and the Freedom Rides

Martin Luther King, the first president of the SCLC, was committed to non-violent struggle.

The Montgomery Bus Boycott — a victory for Integration

Rosa Parks

1) In 1955 in Montgomery, Alabama, Rosa Parks refused to give up her seat on the bus for a white man. She was arrested.
2) Black ministers, led by 26-year-old Martin Luther King, organised a bus boycott in protest. African Americans supported the boycott by walking to work or sharing cars for a year, until the Supreme Court finally ruled that Alabama's bus segregation laws were unconstitutional.
3) The success of this peaceful protest was inspirational to all who opposed segregation in the South.

The Civil Rights Acts of 1957 and 1960 were ineffective

1) The 1957 act created a Civil Rights Commission to investigate obstruction of voting rights.
2) The 1960 act increased record-keeping and supervision of voting procedures.
3) Neither act achieved much in practice, but a small beginning had been made by Congress.

Non-Violent Protest won support

1) Martin Luther King and other activists used peaceful protests like marches, sit-ins and freedom rides (see box below) — gaining publicity and sympathy for the cause.
2) Many peaceful protests were undertaken by civil rights activists:

- In 1960, four African-American students started a series of sit-ins at segregated lunch counters at the Woolworths in Greensboro, North Carolina. These protests spread and some succeeded in forcing the desegregation of facilities.
- The Freedom Rides of 1961, organised by CORE and the SNCC, saw groups of African Americans and white Americans sitting together on bus trips into the South. Segregation on bus services had been ruled unconstitutional by the Supreme Court. There was a violent reaction to the Freedom Rides by some white people in the South — such as the burning of a bus at Anniston, Alabama.

The Birmingham victory convinced the President

1) President Kennedy (who came to power in 1961) at first gave limited support for African-American civil rights. He didn't want to alienate southern white voters.
2) King and the SCLC organised protests in Birmingham, Alabama in April 1963. Protesters were met by police with fire hoses, truncheons and police dogs. Images of the harsh treatment of the protesters in the media gained support for their cause. King and hundreds of others were jailed. But in the end the Birmingham authorities gave way and agreed some concessions.
3) President Kennedy decided it was time to send a major Civil Rights Bill to Congress.

Civil rights — a victory for non-violence...

King was influenced by Gandhi, who used non-violent civil disobedience against the British in India.

Section 13 — Race Relations in the USA 1945-1968

The Civil Rights Struggle in the 1960s

The late 1960s and early 1970s saw the rise of a more <u>confrontational approach</u> to civil rights.

Next came Pressure on Congress

1) In August 1963, 250 000 demonstrators marched on Washington, where King spoke of his <u>dream</u> of a non-racist America.
2) But when Kennedy was <u>assassinated</u> in November 1963, his Civil Rights Bill had still not been passed. He was replaced by President Johnson.
3) Despite the fact that Kennedy was from <u>liberal Massachusetts</u> in the North, and Johnson from <u>segregated Texas</u> in the South, it was Johnson who was more effective in achieving civil rights.

Martin Luther King

Important Acts were passed in 1964 and 1965

1) The <u>Civil Rights Act</u> of <u>1964</u> empowered the Federal Government to <u>enforce desegregation</u> in all public places. This was a big victory for the civil rights movement.
2) <u>Voting rights</u> were still a problem. In theory, African Americans could vote, but in the South all kinds of <u>local rules</u> were invented to stop them.
3) In the 'Freedom Summer' of 1964, thousands of student volunteers spent vacations in Mississippi in a drive for <u>voter registration</u>. Three of these students were <u>murdered</u>.
4) In March 1965 the police in Selma, Alabama, used <u>clubs</u> and <u>tear gas</u> on civil rights marchers and again the brutality was televised. In response, King — who had been awarded the <u>Nobel Peace Prize</u> in 1964 — led a march through Alabama from Selma to Montgomery.
5) In <u>August 1965</u> Johnson signed the <u>Voting Rights Act</u>. Federal registrars would now enforce voting rights. This was another <u>major success</u> for the civil rights movement.

There was still Discrimination and Unrest

1) Formal civil rights <u>weren't enough</u> to help African Americans trapped in <u>poverty</u>.
2) The <u>Vietnam War</u> (see p.92) began to absorb funds which might otherwise have been available for more spending on <u>social programmes</u>.
3) Some African Americans became <u>impatient</u> with King's leadership and <u>non-violent</u> methods.
4) There were many inner-city <u>riots</u> by African Americans in the mid 1960s. 34 people were killed in a 6-day riot in the <u>Watts</u> district of Los Angeles in <u>August 1965</u>. The <u>8-day Detroit riot</u> of <u>July 1967</u> left 43 dead.

Martin Luther King was Assassinated in 1968

1) In <u>1966</u> Martin Luther King went north to <u>Chicago</u> to organise marches against discrimination in <u>housing</u> — a problem not dealt with by the 1964 Civil Rights Act.
2) The government gave no support because President Johnson was angered at the '<u>ingratitude</u>' of black leaders who had <u>criticised</u> his <u>Vietnam War policy</u>.
3) Congress did pass an effective Civil Rights Act for <u>housing</u> after King's <u>assassination</u> in April 1968 had triggered more riots in over 100 <u>cities</u>.

Martin Luther King's death shocked America...

King was <u>shot</u> on a hotel balcony — an escaped prisoner was later convicted of his <u>murder</u>.

The Break with Non-Violence

While Martin Luther King's methods had achieved a great deal, many African Americans were losing patience with the slow pace of reform.

Malcolm X was a convert to the Nation of Islam

1) Malcolm X rejected integration and non-violence. He called the peaceful march on Washington the 'farce on Washington'.
2) His preaching drew converts to the African-American separatist religious organisation, the Nation of Islam. Malcolm X developed more 'inclusive' views and left the Nation of Islam in 1964.
3) He was killed by Nation of Islam members in February 1965.

The SNCC embraced Separatism

1) In 1966 SNCC chairman Stokely Carmichael popularised the 'Black Power' slogan.
2) Under his leadership, the SNCC expelled its white members.
3) In Newark in 1967, after a riot in which over 20 African Americans had been killed by police, a Black Power conference passed resolutions calling for a separate African-American nation and militia.

The Black Panthers went on Patrol

1) The Black Panther Party was founded in 1966 by Huey P. Newton and Bobby Seale.
2) Its members wore uniforms and went on armed patrol, claiming to defend African Americans from police violence.
3) They also carried out programmes providing free breakfasts for children, and education and healthcare for African Americans.

African-American Athletes protested at the Olympics

1) At the 1968 Mexico Olympics two African-American athletes, Tommie Smith and John Carlos, won medals in the men's 200m sprint.
2) During the playing of the national anthem, they bowed their heads and gave the Black Power salute — a raised fist — in protest at the racism and hardship suffered by African Americans back home.
3) The two athletes were thrown out of the Olympic team and sent home. Reaction in the US was largely negative, and the two athletes found later life hard with the notoriety they had gained.
4) The image of the two athletes with raised fists became an important symbol of the Civil Rights struggle.

The Black Panthers — a cat-aclysmic shift in the struggle

Black Power and African-American separatism were frightening developments to many Americans — including those in positions of power. But groups like the Black Panthers also did a lot of good in helping their communities.

Revision Summary

It's another glorious revision summary. It's the usual drill — answer all the questions, then see what you got wrong and revise any weak spots. You'll be an old hand at it by now.

1) What was segregation?

2) Give three examples of facilities where segregation was in force in the South.

3) Who were the Ku Klux Klan?

4) What does NAACP stand for?

5) What was the ruling in the case Brown v Board of Education of Topeka (1954)?

6) Where did Eisenhower send troops in 1957 to enforce school desegregation?

7) What was the name of the African-American student who needed the protection of Federal troops to attend the University of Mississippi?

8) What act of resistance did Rosa Parks make to segregation in 1955?

9) What was the name of the organisation set up in 1957 to investigate the obstruction of African-American voting rights?

10) What protest started in a Woolworths in Greensboro in 1960?

11) What were the Freedom Rides?

12) What major civil rights march happened in 1963?

13) Which President was assassinated in 1963?

14) Who was murdered during the 'Freedom Summer'?

15) Why did the Vietnam War damage programmes designed to help poor African Americans?

16) In which district of LA were there major riots in August 1965?

17) When was Martin Luther King assassinated?

18) How did Malcolm X's approach differ from Martin Luther King's?

19) Who were the founders of the Black Panther Party?

20) What were the names of the athletes who gave the Black Power salute at the 1968 Olympics?

Introduction to the Vietnam War

There's a lot to learn in this topic, so here's a page giving you the rundown on the whole thing.

The First Vietnam War was fought against the French

1) In the 19th century, Vietnam was ruled by the French. During World War Two, a communist group called the Viet Minh were formed — they wanted Vietnam to become independent.

2) Between 1946 and 1954, the Viet Minh fought the French for independence. The USA supported France because they feared that if Vietnam became independent, communism would spread in the Far East. This was known as the 'domino theory'.

3) By 1954, many French forces were based in a military stronghold at Dien Bien Phu. They hoped to draw the Viet Minh into a battle and defeat them once and for all.

4) The Viet Minh attacked but the French had underestimated their strength. After weeks of fighting, the French were defeated and they left Vietnam. The country was split into two — North Vietnam became communist, while South Vietnam had a pro-western, anti-communist government.

Kennedy Increased US Involvement in Vietnam

1) The US had given military help and advice to the French to help prevent the spread of communism.

2) After the split, the US supported the president of South Vietnam, Ngo Dinh Diem, despite the fact that he was very corrupt. The US provided his regime with financial help and political and military advice.

3) In 1960, the communist National Liberation Front was formed in opposition to Diem's government. The military arm of this group became known as the Vietcong.

4) US President Kennedy was determined to stop the spread of communism in Asia. He sent financial aid, military equipment and over 12 000 military advisers to South Vietnam.

The US sent More Troops to Vietnam

1) After Kennedy was assassinated, Lyndon B. Johnson became the new president of the USA.

2) In 1964, US ships were attacked by the North Vietnamese. This became known as the Gulf of Tonkin Incident (see p.95), and it led to full-scale war in Vietnam. President Johnson sent aircraft to attack North Vietnam and ground troops to South Vietnam.

3) By 1965, Johnson increased the number of ground troops to 125 000 men. By 1968 there were over 500 000 US troops in Vietnam.

4) The US troops found it hard fighting the Vietcong in the jungle — so they used tactics such as heavy bombing and chemical weapons instead (see p.94).

5) In 1968, the Vietcong and the North Vietnamese Army (NVA) launched an all-out attack on the South — the Tet Offensive. Although the US recovered most of their losses after three days, fighting continued for several weeks. Eventually, the US defeated the Vietcong and NVA forces.

6) The Tet Offensive was a victory for the US, but it had taken them by surprise, and had led many Americans to oppose the war. After Tet, the new president, Richard Nixon, promised to withdraw US troops from Vietnam and negotiate 'peace with honour'.

The US and Vietnam — in for a penny, in for a pound...

During the 1960s and 1970s, the USA feared the spread of communism. That's what drove the US to support South Vietnam, but the more support it gave, the harder it was to pull out.

The Vietcong

The Vietcong were supported by the NVA — but they weren't a trained army. They weren't as well armed as the US troops, but they turned out to be a tough enemy to fight.

The Vietcong were experienced Guerrilla Fighters

1) Guerrilla warfare is used when small military units want to avoid open battle with a larger, better armed opponent. It involves tactics such as raids and ambushes.
2) The Vietcong were very experienced in guerrilla warfare — the Viet Minh had used guerrilla tactics against Japan and France during World War Two and the First Vietnam War.
3) The Vietcong hoped that guerrilla warfare would exhaust the US troops, lower morale, encourage desertion and encourage South Vietnamese soldiers to defect. The Vietcong wanted the Americans to leave so that they could unify Vietnam as an independent country.

The Vietcong were Hard to Pin Down

The Vietcong used a number of guerrilla tactics that made fighting them very difficult.

1) They worked in small groups and launched surprise attacks on US troops. They knew the land well, so they could choose when and where to attack.
2) In the jungle, they used hidden traps to kill or injure US soldiers. For example, explosives triggered by tripwires and covered pits filled with bamboo spikes.
3) They hid in underground tunnels. These tunnel systems were very complex, and some even had army barracks and hospitals.
4) They blended in easily with Vietnamese villagers. This made it difficult for the US troops to identify Vietcong soldiers.
5) The Vietcong often returned to areas where the US had driven them out. The US army seemed to be making little progress.

The Vietcong's tactics made them strong, but the US army had weaknesses. Most US troops in Vietnam were very young — in their early twenties. Many had been drafted (conscripted) and didn't want to be there. Most only served one year. This gave them little time to gain experience of fighting in the jungle.

The Ho Chi Minh Trail was Crucial for the Vietcong

1) The Ho Chi Minh Trail was a North Vietnamese supply route. It passed through Laos and Cambodia.
2) The trail allowed soldiers, supplies and weapons to be sent from North Vietnam to support the Vietcong in South Vietnam.
3) The trail was used throughout the war and it allowed the Vietcong to keep on fighting.
4) The US tried to bomb the trail but never managed to break it. It was difficult to bomb paths in the jungle as new routes could easily be created. Also, the trail was actually a system of trails which were often added to. Some trails were just decoy routes to confuse the Americans.

The US couldn't fight them if they couldn't find them...

The US had a massive amount of military power, but in the jungle they weren't able to use it to its full potential. Make sure you learn the tactics the Vietcong used and why they were so effective.

Fighting the Vietcong

The US troops needed ways to overcome the Vietcong's guerrilla tactics.

The US launched Major Military Operations

The US used a variety of methods to try to combat the guerrilla tactics of the Vietcong.

Operation Rolling Thunder

1) Operation Rolling Thunder was a huge bombing campaign against North Vietnam which ran from March 1965 until 1968. It was meant to destroy North Vietnam's industry and stop supplies arriving from China.
2) The US hoped that if North Vietnam was weakened, it wouldn't be able to supply the Vietcong.
3) The operation wasn't successful. Vietnam's economy relied on farming, not factories, so it wasn't badly affected. Supplies from China continued to arrive.

'Search and Destroy'

1) 'Search and destroy' was a tactic which focused on killing enemy troops. Instead of securing territory, US forces would simply hunt the Vietcong and clear them out of villages. Villages suspected of supporting the Vietcong were often destroyed. Afterwards, the US troops would move on to another village or return to base.
2) It was difficult to spot Vietcong soldiers from ordinary villagers, so innocent people were sometimes interrogated or even killed. This made the US unpopular.
3) US troops sometimes made brutal attacks to get revenge for their losses. This also made the US unpopular around the world.

Chemical Weapons

1) Napalm was a burning chemical jelly which stuck to people and objects. It was used to destroy hidden targets and burn areas of jungle. It caused many civilian casualties, and its use was widely criticised.
2) Agent Orange was a chemical which destroyed trees and plant life. The US used it to try to remove big parts of the jungle where the Vietcong hid. It was also used to destroy food supplies. It was used on trees and crops, but it was very harmful, and caused cancer and birth defects.

'Hearts and Minds'

1) The US wanted to win South Vietnamese 'hearts and minds', so they wouldn't help the Vietcong.
2) They did this by providing free health care and training programmes for Vietnamese villagers.
3) It wasn't very successful because South Vietnamese civilians had been badly affected by the USA's 'search and destroy' tactics and chemical weapons.
4) The US was also unpopular because it supported the corrupt South Vietnamese government.

'Search and Destroy' led to the My Lai Massacre

1) In March 1968, a 'search and destroy' mission in the village of My Lai led to the murder of over 300 unarmed civilians, including women and children.
2) At first, the US Army tried to cover up the incident — early reports claimed that around 20 civilians had been accidentally killed.
3) But the massacre was revealed by the media in autumn 1969. The news horrified the public and led to a high profile investigation (see p.95).

The conflict in Vietnam had devastating consequences...

Both the Vietcong and the US troops used increasingly brutal tactics as the war raged on. But it was the sheer scale of the damage caused by US tactics that caused the most outrage.

TV and Media Coverage

Hundreds of journalists covered the war in Vietnam. Their reporting was very influential.

Media Coverage led many people to Oppose the War

1) The presence of the media in Vietnam meant that the US public could see what the war was really like.
2) During the 1960s, more and more people owned televisions. A lot of Americans watched news about the war every night, so they knew that the death toll was rising.
3) Reporting was mostly upbeat until the Tet Offensive in 1968 (see p.97). Footage of the Tet Offensive, including scenes showing the Vietcong inside the walls of the US embassy, made many people think that the US was losing the war.
4) A famous photograph from the Tet Offensive shows a South Vietnamese police chief shooting a handcuffed Vietcong soldier in the street. This made many people think that the US and the South Vietnamese were just as brutal as the enemy.
5) Walter Cronkite was a respected news reporter. After the Tet Offensive, Cronkite said that the situation in Vietnam was at a 'stalemate'. His opinions made some US citizens pessimistic about the war.

The Tonkin Incident was Exaggerated

Lyndon B. Johnson

1) On the 2nd August 1964, a US ship, the USS Maddox, was attacked in the Gulf of Tonkin by North Vietnam.
2) Two days later, more attacks on the USS Maddox and the USS Turner Joy were reported. However, there was no proof that these attacks took place.
3) President Johnson announced these suspected attacks, and the story was printed in US newspapers. Johnson made the attacks seem very serious, and he wanted to take action to appear tough.
4) The attacks gave Johnson public and political support for taking further action in Vietnam. Congress (the US parliament) passed the Gulf of Tonkin Resolution, which gave Johnson permission to use 'all necessary steps' to 'prevent further aggression'.
5) In the late 1960s, it was revealed that the second attacks may not have happened. This made many Americans feel that they'd been tricked into the war.

Evidence from My Lai was released in the press

1) In 1968, over 300 Vietnamese civilians were killed in the My Lai Massacre (see p.94). Photographs of the incident were printed in the media in 1969.
2) Public opinion about My Lai was divided — many Americans were horrified by the massacre, and the news increased anti-war feeling. Others believed that the massacre was an unfortunate consequence of the war, and that the My Lai villagers were probably helping the Vietcong.
3) In the early 1970s, several of the soldiers who had taken part in the massacre were brought to trial. Only one officer, Lieutenant William Calley, was convicted. He was sentenced to life in prison, but he was released in 1974.
4) Opinion polls showed that most Americans believed that Calley had just been following orders. Despite this, other polls showed that a majority of Americans opposed the war in Vietnam.

Vietnam — the first TV war...

The media played a crucial role in encouraging people to support the war, and then to oppose it.

Protest Movements

During the 1960s, a strong culture of protest movements developed in the US.

Many Anti-War Demonstrations were held

Chicago Anti-War Protests

1) In 1968, the Democratic Party held its convention in Chicago.
2) The Democrats chose Hubert Humphrey (Johnson's Vice President) as their presidential candidate. Anti-war protestors believed that Humphrey would continue Johnson's Vietnam policies.
3) Violent demonstrations took place and were broadcast on television. 12 000 police and over 5000 National Guardsmen dealt with the protests — over 500 arrests were made.
4) The Republican candidate, Richard Nixon, promised to secure 'peace with honour' in Vietnam, and put an end to the violent protests at home. Nixon won the 1968 election, but it was very close.

Vietnam Veterans' Protest

1) The Vietnam Veterans Against the War (VVAW) was an organisation of soldiers who had fought in Vietnam and wanted the war to end.
2) In April 1971, the VVAW held a week of protests in Washington DC. Over 1000 veterans threw their medals onto the steps of the Capitol — the building where US Congress (parliament) meets.
3) The VVAW protests divided public opinion. Some people felt that Vietnam veterans were worth listening to. Others felt that the demonstrations were unpatriotic.

The Kent State University protest ended in Tragedy

1) Nixon's decision to invade Cambodia (see p.97) sparked off several student protests, including one at Kent State University, Ohio, in May 1970.
2) The Governor of Ohio used the National Guard to deal with the protestors. The students were angry that soldiers had been used and violence broke out.
3) The National Guard used tear gas, and when this didn't disperse the students, they opened fire. Four students were killed. The incident outraged many people and caused riots at other universities across America. Some believed that the protestors were to blame for the outbreak of violence, but some believed that they had a right to protest.

The Fulbright Hearings were a media sensation

1) Senator Fulbright was chairman of the Senate Foreign Relations Committee. Among other things, the committee discussed ways to end the war in Vietnam.
2) In 1971, Fulbright organised a series of hearings from people who both supported and opposed the war. One of the most important testimonies came from John Kerry (a member of the VVAW).
3) In his testimony, Kerry spoke about the Winter Soldier Investigation. In this investigation, several veterans had admitted to committing offences in Vietnam such as rape, torture, and the destruction of entire villages and the people who lived there.
4) The hearings were widely covered in the news. Kerry was the first veteran to speak so publicly about the war and his testimony was a media sensation. Many saw him as a hero for revealing the truth, but others believed he had betrayed the army and the US.

War — what is it good for?

It's difficult to know how most US citizens felt about Vietnam. Despite the large number of protests, President Nixon believed that the 'silent majority' of US citizens supported the war.

Trying to End the War

As the war in Vietnam progressed, it became more and more unpopular in the US.

The Tet Offensive worried the US Public

1) The Tet Offensive (January 1968), was the biggest attack of the war by the Vietcong and the North Vietnamese Army (NVA). Around 80 000 Vietcong troops attacked US bases throughout South Vietnam, including the capital Saigon.

2) The NVA and the Vietcong hoped that the South Vietnamese citizens would join them when they saw the attack and they could force the US out of Vietnam.

3) However, the South Vietnamese did not support the attack. The Vietcong and the NVA were pushed back after three days of fighting. The Vietcong was almost completely destroyed.

4) This was a clear victory for the US. The US Commander, General Westmoreland, believed that the US could soon 'finish the job'.

5) However, the attack had taken the US by surprise. The US public saw images of mass destruction and death. The Tet Offensive made the Vietcong seem strong.

6) Many Americans wanted to end the war. When General Westmoreland requested 200 000 extra soldiers it was very unpopular with the public.

7) President Johnson didn't run for re-election. The new president, Richard Nixon, promised to end the war. He wanted peace without it looking like the US was admitting defeat.

Vietnamisation was Nixon's New Strategy

Richard Nixon

1) Nixon had promised to withdraw US troops from Vietnam. This meant that the South Vietnamese Army (the ARVN) would have to fight the North Vietnamese alone.

2) The US invested money in the ARVN to recruit more troops and provide training and weapons. This was called Vietnamisation.

3) Vietnamisation was largely unsuccessful because ARVN troops lacked discipline. The remaining US troops were also demoralised — they felt that the US wasn't committed to Vietnam, and they were simply waiting to be sent home.

Nixon tried to Pressure North Vietnam to make Peace

Along with Vietnamisation, Nixon used aggressive tactics to force peace talks.

Cambodian Campaign

1) In 1969, Nixon began a bombing campaign in Cambodia to try to destroy the Ho Chi Minh Trail and pressure North Vietnam to make peace.

2) He also sent in 30 000 US ground troops to destroy communist bases and supplies.

3) However, crossing into Cambodia led to more anti-war demonstrations (see p.96).

4) Anti-war feeling led Congress to cut military spending and cancel the Gulf of Tonkin Resolution (see p.95). This made it difficult for Nixon to carry on the war.

Laos Campaign

1) In 1971 the South Vietnamese Army attacked the Ho Chi Minh Trail in Laos.

2) US troops couldn't enter Laos, but they provided air support.

3) Although many communist supplies were destroyed, the South Vietnamese army was quickly driven out of Laos.

President Nixon — bombing his way to peace...

Nixon hoped that heavy bombing would pressure North Vietnam into signing a peace agreement.

Peace and Defeat

A peace deal for Vietnam took a <u>long time to negotiate</u>, and the peace <u>didn't last</u> very long...

Initial Peace Talks were Unsuccessful

1) <u>Peace talks</u> with North Vietnam were first held in <u>Paris</u> in <u>1968</u>, under President Johnson. In <u>1969</u>, Nixon also held <u>secret</u> peace talks — but both were <u>unsuccessful</u>.
2) North Vietnam was in <u>no hurry</u> to make peace, and it <u>refused</u> to <u>withdraw its troops</u> from South Vietnam. The North Vietnamese government believed that <u>anti-war protests</u> in the US and military <u>spending cuts</u> would soon <u>force Nixon</u> to make <u>peace</u>.

Peace was agreed at the Paris Peace Conference

On <u>27th January 1973</u> both sides signed the <u>Paris Peace Accords</u>. The key agreements were:

- The president of South Vietnam, <u>General Thieu</u>, could stay in power.
- The <u>NVA</u> could <u>stay</u> in areas of South Vietnam which it already <u>controlled</u>.
- All <u>US prisoners of war</u> would be <u>released</u>.
- All <u>US troops</u> would <u>leave Vietnam</u> within <u>two months</u>.

Both sides wanted to Reach a Deal

North Vietnam

1) The US had <u>improved</u> its <u>relations</u> with <u>China</u> and the <u>USSR</u>. These countries were North Vietnam's <u>allies</u>. They <u>encouraged</u> North Vietnam to make <u>peace</u>.
2) In December 1972, the US launched its '<u>Christmas bombing</u>' of North Vietnam. The renewed bombing made North Vietnam eager for the US to leave.
3) The North Vietnamese government wanted a chance to <u>recover</u> and <u>rebuild</u>, and then mount a <u>final assault</u> on South Vietnam.

USA

1) The war was becoming <u>increasingly unpopular</u> in the US.
2) It was <u>difficult to finance</u> the war after Congress cut military spending.
3) It seemed the war would <u>drag on</u> for a long time.

The Fall of Saigon showed that Peace had Failed

1) US troops were <u>gradually</u> being withdrawn from 1969, but once the <u>peace treaty</u> was signed, <u>all remaining troops</u> left Vietnam.
2) By <u>1974</u> the US had withdrawn all its <u>troops</u>, and Congress had stopped all <u>financial help</u> to the country as well — South Vietnam was left to <u>defend itself</u>.
3) North Vietnam <u>invaded</u> South Vietnam in <u>late 1974</u>. They advanced rapidly against the <u>weak</u> and disorganised South Vietnamese forces. In <u>April 1975</u>, they took control of the South Vietnamese capital, Saigon.
4) Helicopters landed on the roof of the <u>US embassy</u> to pick up the last remaining diplomats. This <u>evacuation</u> was broadcast <u>on television</u>. Many Americans who watched it felt that the chaotic scenes were an <u>embarrassment</u> for their country.

Saigon, 1975 — a not quite honourable exit...

Some argued that the US evacuation was a <u>success</u>, with thousands of people lifted to safety. Others believed it was <u>chaotic</u> and <u>disorganised</u> and that evacuation should have begun <u>earlier</u>.

Revision Summary

Now is not the time to admit defeat. Now is the time to take on the challenge of answering these fearsome revision summary questions. Okay, they're not as fearsome as the Vietcong, but they're surely fearsome enough to prepare you for your History exam.

1) Where were the French finally defeated in the First Vietnamese War?
2) What was the name of the military arm of the National Liberation Front?
3) What was the name of the type of warfare that the Vietcong used?
4) Name two tactics used by the Vietcong.
5) What was the name of the supply route that connected North and South Vietnam?
6) Name two chemical weapons used in the war and describe their effects.
7) What were the two main aims of 'Operation Rolling Thunder'?
8) How did the US try to win over the 'hearts and minds' of the Vietnamese people?
9) Which US news reporter said that the US and North Vietnam were in a 'stalemate' following the Tet Offensive?
10) What was the Gulf of Tonkin incident?
11) What was the name of the massacre that journalists revealed in 1969?
12) What was the name of the only soldier convicted for his part in the massacre?
13) What does VVAW stand for?
14) At which US university were four students killed in anti-war protests in May 1970?
15) Why was John Kerry's testimony so important?
16) Who became the new US president in 1968?
17) What was the name of the offensive the Vietcong and the North Vietnamese army launched in January 1968?
18) What was Vietnamisation and why was it unsuccessful?
19) President Nixon extended the war into which country in 1970?
20) How did the US support the South Vietnamese Army in the Laos Campaign?
21) Give two reasons why the North Vietnamese government were willing to make a ceasefire deal in 1973.
22) In which year did the North Vietnamese army take control of Saigon?

How to Study History

You've learnt the <u>facts</u> — now you need to learn how to <u>use them</u> effectively.
There are <u>four key ideas</u> that'll help you use your facts — the four 'C's: Cause, Consequence, Change and Continuity.

You'll get questions about Causes and Consequences

1) <u>Cause</u> means the <u>reason</u> something happened — e.g. the causes of the First World War. Any time you have an event in History, think about <u>what</u> caused it and <u>why</u> it happened. There are always reasons why an event takes place and it's your job to work them out.

2) <u>Consequence</u> means what happened <u>because</u> of an action — it's the <u>result</u> of an event, e.g. a consequence of the Second World War was that the USA and USSR became superpowers because the big powers in Europe were then too weak.

> 1) Some questions will ask you to give an <u>opinion</u> about causes and consequences — e.g. 'The Great Depression was the main cause of the failure of the League of Nations — do you agree?' or 'Which was a more important factor in ending communism in the USSR — glasnost or perestroika?'.
>
> 2) It's up to you what <u>opinion</u> you give — but you've got to be able to <u>back it up</u> with <u>reasons</u> and <u>facts</u>.
>
> 3) With this type of question, it's good to look at the different <u>causes / consequences</u> — and then explain which you think was the <u>most important</u> and <u>why</u>.

You also need to think about Change and Continuity

1) <u>Change</u> is when something happens to make things <u>different</u> — there can be <u>quick</u> changes, e.g. the assassination of Archduke Franz Ferdinand contributed to the outbreak of the First World War. Or there can be <u>slow</u> changes, e.g. the tensions between Britain and Germany in the early 1900s were a long-term factor leading to the start of the First World War.

2) <u>Continuity</u> is the <u>opposite</u> of change — it means when things stay the <u>same</u>, e.g. the Romanov dynasty ruled Russia for 300 years.

3) These ideas are opposites — think of <u>continuity</u> as a <u>flat line</u> going along until there is a sudden <u>change</u> and the line becomes a <u>zigzag</u>:

CONTINUITY   **CHANGE**

> Use the four 'C's in your answers — <u>link facts</u> together and tell the examiners <u>why</u> something happened and what the <u>results</u> were. <u>Explain</u> if there was a change and if so, what things changed from and what they changed to.

Time for some exam tips...

Obviously, you're going to need to <u>learn</u> all the info for your topics. But to get <u>high marks</u>, you need to do more than just trot out the facts. You need to be able to discuss topics in a thoughtful way, showing good understanding. The four 'C's are really useful for this.

Handling Sources

There are few certainties in life — but you will get <u>source questions</u> in your exam...

There are Two main kinds of Sources

1) <u>Primary sources</u> — this is evidence <u>from</u> the period you're studying, e.g. a newspaper report on the First World War from 4th September 1914.

2) <u>Secondary sources</u> — this is evidence <u>about</u> a historical period, e.g. a 1989 book entitled 'Origins of the First World War'.

Sources may be <u>visual extracts</u>, e.g. photographs and maps, or <u>written extracts</u>, e.g. diaries, newspapers etc.

If you want to Do Well look at sources Carefully

1) You've got to find <u>evidence</u> from the source which is <u>relevant</u> to the question.
2) Show you <u>understand</u> the source, and use the facts you already know about the period to <u>explain</u> what the source is saying, and <u>how</u> it says it.
3) Say <u>how reliable and useful</u> you think the source is. Think about whether the source gives <u>enough</u> information about the topic or if there are <u>gaps</u> or <u>inconsistencies</u>. Say if you think the source is <u>biased</u> (one-sided in its opinions) — and if so, why.

> Don't confuse facts and opinions — always think about <u>who</u> is writing, <u>why</u> they are writing and <u>what</u> they are trying to say.

Top Tips for answering source questions

Do

1) <u>Use</u> the source material to help answer the question — not just what you know already.
2) <u>Read</u> the question <u>carefully</u>. E.g. if it says to use the three sources A, B and C, you must use all three.
3) Check what the source tells you — look out for <u>what</u> a source says, <u>who</u> wrote it and <u>when</u> they wrote it.
4) If you're asked to look at more than one source, then <u>compare them</u>.
5) Use the <u>facts you already know</u> about the period to <u>help you understand</u> the source and judge how useful it is.

Don't

1) Don't get carried away writing down everything you know about the topic — <u>focus</u> on the source(s) given.
2) <u>Don't jump to conclusions</u> — e.g. don't assume that every eyewitness account is accurate.
3) <u>Don't</u> always take sources at <u>face value</u>. E.g. a history book about the Russian Revolution that was written in Stalin's USSR might <u>exaggerate</u> his role and <u>leave out</u> people like Trotsky.

Historians love ketchup — they're obsessed with sources...

Evaluating sources is an <u>important skill</u> for historians — and one you have to demonstrate in the exam. So if you want decent grades, put the effort into learning this page right now.

Exam Essay Skills

You've also got to be able to tackle <u>essay answers</u>...

Planning *Your Exam Time*

1) On the exam paper, it'll say next to each question <u>how many marks</u> it's worth.
2) Look out for which questions have <u>most marks</u> — make sure you spend <u>most time</u> on these.
3) There'll be at least one or two questions which require <u>essay-length</u> answers.

> <u>Learn the rule</u> — the <u>more marks</u> a question is worth, the <u>longer</u> your answer should be. Don't get carried away writing loads for a question that's only worth 4 marks — you need to <u>leave time</u> for the higher mark questions.

Remember these Three Tips *for writing good* Essays

1) *Plan your Essay*

<u>Sort out</u> what you want to say before you start writing — think about <u>how to answer the question</u>, and what the <u>key words</u> are. Scribble a <u>quick plan</u> of your main points — <u>cross through this neatly</u> at the end, so it's obvious it shouldn't be marked.

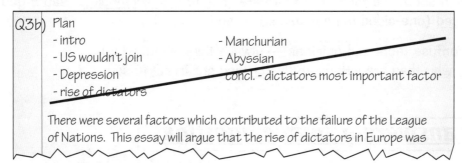

Q3b) Plan
- intro
- US wouldn't join
- Depression
- rise of dictators
- Manchurian
- Abyssian
concl. - dictators most important factor

There were several factors which contributed to the failure of the League of Nations. This essay will argue that the rise of dictators in Europe was

2) *Stay Focused* on the Question

Make sure that you <u>directly answer the question</u>. <u>Back up your points</u> with relevant facts. Don't just chuck in everything you know. You've got to be <u>relevant</u> and <u>accurate</u> — e.g. if you're writing about the rise of the Nazi Party, don't include stories about a London camel called George who moved rubble during the Blitz.

3) *Use a Clear* Writing Style

Your essay should start with a brief <u>introduction</u> and end with a <u>conclusion</u>. Remember to start a <u>new paragraph</u> for each new point you want to discuss. Try to use <u>clear handwriting</u> — and pay attention to <u>spelling</u>, <u>grammar</u> and <u>punctuation</u> (see p.103-106).

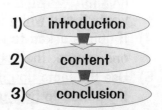

1) introduction
2) content
3) conclusion

There's no need to panic in the exam...

Even if you've revised properly, remembered a spare pen and arrived early for your exam, there's a chance you'll suffer from 'mind blank syndrome' when you open the paper. But don't panic, just stay calm, <u>read the questions carefully</u>, and <u>use the advice</u> you've learnt here.

Spelling, Punctuation and Grammar

You get marks in your exams for having good <u>SPaG</u> (spelling, punctuation and grammar).
This stuff might not be particularly thrilling but if you can get it right, it's <u>easy marks</u>.

Remember *to Check* what you've Written

1) Leave <u>5 minutes</u> at the end of the exam to <u>check your work</u>.

2) 5 minutes <u>isn't</u> long, so there <u>won't</u> be time to check <u>everything</u> thoroughly.
   Look for the <u>most obvious</u> spelling, punctuation and grammar <u>mistakes</u>.

3) <u>Start</u> by checking your answers to the questions which award <u>SPaG marks</u>.
   There'll be instructions on the exam paper telling you which these are.
   <u>Only</u> check the rest of your answers if you've got <u>time</u>.

Check for common *Spelling Mistakes*

When you're writing under pressure, it's <u>easy</u> to let <u>spelling</u>
<u>mistakes</u> creep in, but there are a few things you can watch out for:

Check for missing words as well as misspelt words.

1) Look out for words which <u>sound the same</u> but <u>mean different things</u> and are <u>spelt differently</u>.
   Make sure you've used the correct one. For example, 'their', 'they're' and 'there':

The Bolsheviks had <u>their</u> own military force known as the Red Guards.	During hyperinflation, bank notes can lose so much value that <u>they're</u> practically worthless.	Under Tsar Nicholas II <u>there</u> were food shortages, demonstrations and strikes.

2) <u>Don't</u> use text speak, and always write words out <u>in full</u>. For example, use '<u>and</u>' instead of '<u>&</u>' or '<u>+</u>'. <u>Don't</u> use 'etc.' when you could give <u>more examples</u> or a <u>better explanation</u>.

3) Make sure you've used the appropriate <u>technical terms</u> (like 'collectivisation' or 'détente'). If they're <u>spelt correctly</u>, it'll really <u>impress</u> the <u>examiner</u>.

Make sure your *Grammar* and *Punctuation* are *Correct*

1) Check you've used <u>capital letters</u>, <u>full stops</u> and <u>question marks</u> correctly (see p.106).

2) Make sure your writing <u>isn't too chatty</u> and doesn't use <u>slang words</u>. It should be <u>formal</u>.

3) Watch out for sentences where your writing switches between <u>different</u>
   <u>tenses</u>. You should usually stick to <u>one tense</u> throughout your answer
   (don't worry if you quote from a source that's in a different tense).

4) Check that you've started a <u>new paragraph</u> every time you make a new point.
   It's important that your answer <u>isn't</u> just <u>one long block</u> of text (see p.106).

5) Watch out for tricksy little <u>grammar mistakes</u>:

   • Remember — '<u>it's</u>' (with an apostrophe) is short for '<u>it is</u>' or '<u>it has</u>'.
     '<u>Its</u>' (without an apostrophe) means '<u>belonging to it</u>'.

   • It's always '<u>should have</u>', not 'should of' (and also 'could have' and 'would have' too).

   If you know that you <u>often</u> confuse two words, like 'it's' and 'its',
   <u>watch out</u> for them when you're checking your work in the exam.

Check, check, check, goose, check, check, check...

It's really useful to practise all this stuff <u>before</u> the exam if you can. That way it'll become
second nature — you'll do it all automatically and make <u>fewer errors</u> in the first place. Hurrah.

Spelling, Punctuation and Grammar

Making a mistake in your exam is <u>not</u> the end of the world, so don't panic if you find one.
If you just cross it out <u>neatly</u> and correct the mistake, you <u>won't</u> lose any marks at all.

Make your corrections Neatly

1) If the mistake is just <u>one word</u> or a <u>short phrase</u>, cross it
out <u>neatly</u> and write the correct word <u>above</u> it.

> Communist party members loyal to Stalin ~~recieved~~ ^{received} privileges such as holidays.

2) If you've <u>forgotten</u> to start a <u>new paragraph</u>, use a <u>double strike</u>
(like this '//') to show where the new paragraph should <u>begin</u>:

> *See p.106 for more on paragraphs.*

If only someone had told Graham about the double strike.

> Collectivisation helped peasants work together and provided large-scale organisation
> for food production. **//** However, the new system was not very successful at first.
> Many people died of starvation after a bad harvest caused a serious famine, which was
> made worse by the kulaks, who had started to destroy crops and animals in protest.

Use an Asterisk to add Extra Information

1) If you've <u>missed something out</u>, decide if you have space to write the missing bit <u>above</u>
the line you've already written. If you <u>can</u>, use a ' ^ ' to show <u>exactly where</u> it should go.

> Civil rights issues became a particular focus in 1955, with the Montgomery bus boycott.
> Rosa Parks was arrested for refusing to give up her bus seat for a white man. Martin
> Luther King reacted by organising a ^{bus}boycott with other black ministers. The success
> of their peaceful protest was inspirational to everyone who opposed segregation.

2) If the bit you've missed out <u>won't</u> fit above the line, use an <u>asterisk</u>
(like this '*') to show the examiner <u>where</u> the missing bit should go.

3) Write the <u>missing words</u> at the <u>end</u> of your answer with another asterisk next to them.

> The Treaty of Versailles was very harsh on Germany. A lot of land* was confiscated
> and Germany was forced by Article 231 to accept the blame for the war.
>   *including Alsace and Lorraine

Cross Out anything you Don't want to be Marked

1) If you've written something that you <u>don't</u> want the examiner to mark, <u>cross it out neatly</u>.

2) Cross out any <u>notes</u>. If you don't <u>finish</u> your answer <u>in time</u>, don't cross out your <u>plan</u> —
the examiner might look at it to see what you were <u>going to write</u>.

3) Don't <u>scribble things out</u> without thinking — it'll make your answers look <u>messy</u>.

When making corrections, neatness is the name of ^{the}^game

Examiners love it if your answer is <u>neat</u> and <u>tidy</u> — it makes it super easy for them to read.
This means they can spend more time giving you lots of <u>marks</u> for the great stuff you've written.

Spelling, Punctuation and Grammar

Some words are darn tricky to spell. There's no way around them — you need to learn them off by heart. This page has some of the most common ones you'll need for your history exams.

Learn these Useful Words

The underlined words are useful in a lot of answers, so you need to know how to spell them.

> There were many arguments in the Supreme Court over Roosevelt's New Deal.

> The Nazis were successful at controlling people through fear and propaganda.

> The US didn't join the League of Nations because they believed it would lead to new wars.

> In July 1917, the Bolsheviks attempted to take control of the government.

> The Wall Street Crash affected companies across the world.

> American banks were encouraged to lend money to lots of businesses in the 1920s.

> There are many differences between the New Economic Policy and War Communism.

Spell Technical Words Correctly

There are a lot of technical words in History. You need to be able to spell them correctly.
Learn these examples to start you off. The coloured letters are the tricky bits to watch out for.

agriculture	constitution	evidence	parliament
alliance	defence	fascism	rebellion
biased	democracy	foreign	reliability
conflict	diplomacy	league	resistance
controversial	effective	military	source

You'll also have to learn how to spell the names and technical terms from the options you're studying. So for The USSR 1924-41 you'll need to be comfortable with names like 'Zinoviev' and terms such as 'Bolshevik'. Go back through the options you've studied and make a list of tricky names and words — then learn them.

Learn this page and make spelling errors history...

Mnemonics can help you remember how to spell tricky words. For example, you can remember 'biased' with the phrase 'Bleary Insomniacs Avoid Sleep Every Day'. Or something similar...

Spelling, Punctuation and Grammar

You need to Punctuate Properly...

1) Always use a capital letter at the start of a sentence.
   Use capital letters for names of particular people, places and things. For example:

   All sentences start → In 1933 Hitler was made Chancellor of Germany.
   with capital letters.

   The name of a person.　A title.　The name of a country.

2) Full stops go at the end of sentences, e.g. 'Franz Ferdinand was killed in June 1914.'
   Question marks go at the end of questions, e.g. 'How successful was the New Deal?'

3) Use commas when you use more than one adjective, or to separate items in a list:

   Hitler envisioned a highly militarised, racially superior German nation.

   Lenin's April Theses promised peace, bread, land and freedom.

4) Commas can join two points into one sentence with a joining word (e.g. 'and', 'so' or 'but'):

   Hitler wanted to make Germany self-sufficient, so it didn't depend on foreign imports.

   Hoover tried to help big business, but he didn't do enough to help ordinary people.

5) Commas can also be used to separate extra information in a sentence:

   Tsar Nicholas II, who had absolute power in Russia, became increasingly unpopular throughout his reign.

   The Ku Klux Klan, a group which believed in white supremacy, used violence to intimidate African Americans.

   When you use commas like this, the sentence should still make sense when the extra bit is taken out.

...and use Grammar Correctly

1) Don't change tenses in your writing by mistake:

   Some business people were angry that the New Deal allowed trade unions into the workplace.

   Both verbs are in the past tense — which is correct. Writing 'allows' instead of 'allowed' would be wrong.

2) Don't use double negatives. You should only use a negative once in a sentence:

   Collectivisation was enforced by law; Russian peasants did not have any choice.

   Don't put 'no' here.

3) Write longer answers in paragraphs. A paragraph is a group of sentences which talk about the same thing or follow on from each other. Start a new paragraph when you make a new point. Show a new paragraph by starting a new line and leaving a gap before you start writing:

   This gap shows a new paragraph.

   From 1933 Hitler started a programme of public works, such as the building of huge new motorways. This gave jobs to thousands of people.
   　　Even though there was increased employment, the Nazis altered the statistics so that things looked better than they were. Wages were also poor.

   Remember that you should start a new paragraph for each of your main points.

Phew, now you're fully SPaG-ed and ready to go...

You should now be ready to tackle any History essay that comes your way...

Index

Index